"Writing is all about revelation, whether the new author understands that or not. Dr. Hunter's book, Write Your Memoir, *gives fair warning to those just beginning to explore the dark recesses and sunlit plains of personal stories. The journey is an amazing one, and Hunter is a remarkable guide."*

—*Nora Klaver,*
author of Mayday!: Asking for Help in Times of Need

"The beauty of this book is in the way it takes its followers well beyond the writing process and into a deeper, spiritual journey. Not satisfied with merely getting the story right, Allan Hunter holds the writer to a higher cause, a deeper challenge – that of transformation. This book is about our relationship to our selves, our relationship to our lives; it is about deepening those relationships through the daily devotion and discipline of writing. Allan Hunter's wisdom and discernment of the process of growth and transformation is woven throughout, bringing to us the tools we need to do the soul work of memoir writing. What a gift he has given to those of us dedicated to telling the truth, and in telling it, finding it; that is, learning what – in fact – our personal truths really are."

—*Connie D. Griffin,*
author of To Tell the Truth: Practice and Craft in Narrative Nonfiction

D0052466

Other Books by Allan G. Hunter:

Stories We Need to Know
The Six Archetypes of Love
Princes, Frogs & Ugly Sisters
The Sanity Manual
From Coastal Command to Captivity

Write Your Memoir

The soul work of telling your story

Dr. Allan G. Hunter

FINDHORN PRESS

The right of Allan G. Hunter to be identified as the author of this work
has been asserted by him in accordance with the Copyright, Designs and
Patents Act 1998.

First published by Findhorn Press 2010

ISBN: 978-1-84409-177-5

British Library Cataloguing-in-Publication Data.
A catalogue record for this book is available from the British Library.

Edited by Jane Engel
Cover design by Damian Keenan
Layout by PrePress-Solutions.com
Printed and bound in USA

1 2 3 4 5 6 7 8 9 10 11 12 13 14 15 14 13 12 11 10

Published by
Findhorn Press
305A The Park,
Findhorn, Forres
Scotland IV36 3TE

Tel +44(0)1309 690582
Fax +44(0)1309 690036
eMail info@findhornpress.com
www.findhornpress.com

Contents

Acknowledgments

There are many people I wish to thank and all have been helpful in very different ways. My gratitude goes first and foremost to Robert Atwan, General Editor of the *Best American Essays* series, whose inspiration was the starting point for the Blue Hills Writing Institute at Curry College. Without his vision I would never have gone so deeply into the challenges of teaching of Memoir, and so this book would never have come about. Others amongst my colleagues were also influential, and they include Rea Cassidy, Dr. David Fedo, Dr. Connie Griffin, Sandy Kaye, Rebecca McClanahan, Suzanne Strempek Shea (who deserves a special mention), and Dennis Watlington. Support of an administrative nature came from Dr. Lisa Ijiri, Dr. Susan Pennini, Dr. David Potash, Dr. Ruth Sherman, Dr. Judy Stoessel, Steven Beliaef, and Catherine Kemp Sawyer. I'd also like to make special mention of Kenny Wightman and Suzie Hackett, who helped me explore memoir's more intricate aspects, and did so with grace and generosity. In addition I'd like to mention my late father, who allowed me to work with him on the memoir that later became *From Coastal Command to Captivity*. Without that experience I might not have been alerted to the ways memoir can effect change at a deep level.

My students, some of whom provided the examples that illustrate this book, and many of whom have now become my friends, were more influential than perhaps they know. My particular thanks go to Madeleine Biondolillo, Vivian Brock, Perry Carrison, Laura Cluff, Ruth Cote, Samantha Crescitelli, Brittany Capozzi, Jane O'Connor Deering, Marlena Erdos, Virginia Fuller, Patricia Horwitz, Emma Lown, Alison McLeod, Marilyn Morrissey, Jean Mudge, Alyssa Newton, Ed Orzechowski, Holly Pappas, Jane Perkins, Tel Sandman, Janet Sedgewick, Mary Lou Shields, Diane Snyder, and Cheryl Suchors. If I have missed anyone out I can only apologize and say that it was simply not possible to list everyone here, much as I would have wished to.

To my friends and colleagues who have given such valuable feedback when reading my work I owe a debt of gratitude, too, and these include Professor David

Whitley of Cambridge University; Andrew Peerless of Oxford University Press, Professors Andrew Horn, Jeffrey Di Iuglio, Jeanette de Jong, and Veronica Guerrero-Macia; to Dr. Laurie Fox, Dr. Peter Hainer, Dr. Bette Manter, Dr. Alan Revering, and Dr. Ronald Warners, all of Curry College; and to my good friends Susan Lax and Douglas Kornfeld, Talbot Lovering and Tina Forbes, Kelly Ferry, and Dr. Martha Duncan. Kaetlyn Wilcox, an extraordinary artist, was generous in providing details of her artistic process that were of real assistance in explaining what happens as we piece together our lives to make sense of it all. Sandie Sedgebeer at *Inspired Parenting Magazine* and Vara Raleigh at *PlanetLightWorker* were instrumental in keeping the ideas that make up this book flowing. Writing truly is a practice and writing a regular column for these publications helped my creative juices to remain vital – and was also a lot of fun.

My wife, Catharine Bennett, deserves special mention as without her support and love and deep wisdom shared over many conversations nothing would ever have been written.

A heartfelt thank you goes to Thierry Bogliolo for his kindness and support of my writing, as well as his belief in the power of books to make the world a better place. I could not ask to find a better publisher nor a more delightful and more cherished friend. To Jane Engel, my editor at Findhorn Press, to Carol Shaw, and to the whole Findhorn team a huge thank you. And to Gail Torr, surely the finest publicist anyone could ever wish for, gratitude, gratitude, and still more gratitude.

I was materially assisted in preparing this book by the generosity of President Kenneth Quigley of Curry College, and the Board of Trustees, who granted me a sabbatical in Spring 2008 during which this book was planned, as well as allowing me Release Time for 2010 to bring the task to completion. I am also grateful to the trustees of the Seth Sprague Educational and Charitable Foundation, and especially Mrs. Arline Greenleaf and Mrs. Rebecca Greenleaf Clapp, as their continued support of the Curry College Honors Program has not only enabled that program to flourish, but also has also permitted me to be able to engage students with questions about identity that, to a large extent, lie at the core of this book. My students' learning and mine has intersected in a way that has been beneficial to all concerned, and this could not have happened without such generous support.

Last but not least I would like to thank those who patiently put up with me during this time of writing, particularly my family: Billie Bennett, Grant Bennett and Emily Tabacoff, Nicholas Portnoy, Anna Portnoy, Don and Annatje Hunter, Betty Moorley, Alison and Kenny Portas, Hussein Khan and Maria Szebor, and Monique and Martin Lowe, all of whom gave excellent advice and insights, and were more supportive than they may realize.

Disclaimer

The intention of this work is to instruct and educate writers and readers who wish to explore memoir writing. If the writing exercises cause you the reader emotional distress then I urge you to seek professional help. This book cannot on its own be a substitute for counseling or therapy.

The examples in this book are all actual examples that have been shared in classes and workshops. I have secured permissions from all those I have quoted directly, and in these instances some writers have allowed me to use their real names. To protect the privacy of all the individuals concerned, and in the interests of compression, I have on occasion altered certain facts and details while remaining true to the spirit of the events described.

For my mother, with love

Chapter One

What is Soul Work? What does it look like? Why is it Worth Doing?

So you've decided to start a memoir. Good. This book will help you in that process. It won't be prescriptive – it won't tell you what you must have and where in the text you must have it. Instead it will take you through a series of exercises and writing activities, all of which are designed to bring memories to light, and to do so in a new way. And it will ask you to listen to yourself in all this, so that you can decide what needs to be in your memoir, and what shape it needs to take. For this will be an individual choice for each writer. There are no cookie-cutters here. One size will not fit all. And so as we go through this book I'll ask you to take the time to do the exercises; if this process is to work properly you cannot just think about doing them, you'll actually have to put pen to paper (or fingers to keyboard) and write. In this way you'll learn to value the memories you have and allow them speak to you. Only then can they reveal their deep meaning to you – the meaning you've been looking for.

For the past thirty years I've spent a considerable amount of time with people young and old as they write about their lives, getting them to tell their stories in the ways that feel most authentic to each of them. What has become clear over that time is that writing about one's life, or better still, writing the story of one's life, causes change at a deep level. So profound is this process that it seems to be best described as Soul Work, since it moves each writer into a different relationship to him or herself and to the past. If you take on this work it will also alter your relationship to the world around you, which in turn provides an enhanced sense of what matters most in life. It's a spiritual process, although it might not look like it when one watches a writer, day after day, at the desk.

Writing one's life story involves a process that most people don't quite understand. To explain I'll give you a comparison. In Andrei Tarkovsky's wonderful movie *The Sacrifice*, which he made as he was dying of cancer, there is a minor character - a small boy who is seen everyday walking over a barren landscape lugging a bucket of water, which he pours over the base of a very dead-looking tree. People tell him it's useless, but he keeps popping into the frame, barely strong enough to carry the bucket and does it anyway. The other characters shake their heads and sigh, busy with their confusions and arguments. Almost the last scene in the movie shows the boy still dragging the bucket up the hill, except now the tree has green buds and leaves on it.

As a metaphor for Tarkovsky's hope that the then Soviet Union would eventually change, it works well and all the more eerily so since the Soviet tyranny did in fact collapse a few years later, after Tarkovsky was dead. As a metaphor for quiet belief in daily devotion to a task it works also. The filmmaker must have felt he was rather like the small boy, trying to coax an uninterested world intent on its absurd arms race to turn back to life and to living. And from our point of view it has deep resonance too – turning up every day to write one's life story may look to some like a losing proposition, but in the doing of it something changes within the writer. Dead trees sprout leaves, one's sense of life is enriched – and we move closer to an awareness of what our lives might mean.

Knowing this can be a great help as we set out along this seemingly daunting path. Perhaps you will sell your script and make a fortune. That would be delightful. But the first consideration should not be money or readership. It should be that this is work you need to do for yourself.

In some ways, if you are reading this, you are already at that point of change. Deciding to write your memoir means you are already moving into a different relationship to your life experiences. We all have 'stories' that we tell ourselves about our lives. Some of these stories are conscious (such as I'm a white male, or that someone else is an Italian female) and some of them may be less conscious, such as when we may tend to act, at times, like victims, or to accept less than we are due, or when we tell ourselves, 'I never have any luck in this aspect of my life.' We know some of our stories; others are waiting to be known. When you decide to write your memoir you are saying two things. The first is that you believe you have a story that's worth sharing. The second is that in sharing it you believe there is some inner value that you are trying to express that can only be conveyed fully by telling that story. Your 'take' on the world has value and its ultimate worth also may need to be clarified to you, yourself, through the process of writing it out. This is a little like the difference between the magnificent memo to the boss that you compose at night, lying awake, that is a masterpiece of tact and intelligence, and the actual memo you send, knowing that it will be read in the real world. The first is abstract, operating in a world that you have temporarily created. The second – well, the second version means you actually have to take responsibility for your words.

Each of us has a life story waiting to make its way into the light of day. And there's no better time to start than right now.

So let's think about this for a moment. Life comes at us at different speeds. Sometimes it comes so fast we don't have time to record anything, and we have no opportunity to get things straight in our minds before the next event hurries along. Sometimes it comes at us so slowly that we think nothing much is happening until, much later, we look back and see that in fact a huge amount was going on. Ask any parent of small children – even one who keeps a diary every day without fail – and you'll get the same answer. The child who was crawling starts to walk, and the parent's life is never the same again. Since this is the case, how can we even attempt to record all the events that happen to us in a coherent fashion?

Yet if we can't or don't take the time to record what happens in our lives then it becomes very hard to make sense of chronology, to keep track of events, and ultimately it becomes almost impossible to understand them. Which of us hasn't found ourselves, at some time or another in our lives, looking back at an event and saying that we really didn't see that one coming? Or perhaps we find ourselves not knowing how we got to this particular difficulty. How did my life get to this point? If we can't remember the steps we went through we'll find it very hard to understand how we got to our present moment.

At various points in our lives we'll want to do just that; we'll want to try and reconstruct the past in order to make sense of it. Perhaps you have reached a turning point in your life and you feel the need to reassess what has been going on. Marriage, graduation, divorce, moving house or changing jobs, the birth of a child, retirement, the arrival of grandchildren, bereavements, a near-death experience – any and all of these events, and others, can move us to the place of contemplation and wonder.

This sort of reassessment is not simply idle or nostalgic, although some people just shrug it off as too complicated to think about. If you allow yourself to review what has happened in your life you'll be engaged in what I call soul work. It deserves to be taken seriously. If we do the necessary reflecting we can make connections, become more thoughtful, and access our understanding. We can grow our souls and transform our hearts. We can expand our wisdom and our compassion. In fact the very act of wanting to understand is never simply based in idle curiosity: it's always a desire to look beneath the surface of things, to find the deep structures that make up our psyches.

Many people don't know this, at least to begin with. Most think that they've been through a difficult series of circumstances and they feel the need to get it on paper, somehow. Others feel that they've had interesting lives and they want to write it all down. These are good places to start from. And for everyone who does make a start there is the opportunity to do some profound soul work. Still other writers feel a driving need to communicate what they have lived through.

Elie Wiesel described this best when he wrote, "It is the duty of the survivor to speak of his experience and share it with his friends and contemporaries." Wiesel was a survivor of the Nazi concentration camps, so he knew that sharing his experiences was not just a form of self-indulgence. He wanted to warn others so the events he'd lived through would never occur again. The word he uses, 'duty' is an important one. To some extent we owe it to others, and to ourselves, to tell our stories.

Almost every writer I've worked with has realized in the course of writing that this was work that could enrich the understanding of what life is, and what it could be. Here's what one of my students wrote, echoing the thoughts of others: "I write because somehow, when I'm doing it, I begin to see the shapes and patterns of my life, and it begins to make sense to me." (Mara M.)

This recognition of what one is doing at a deep level sometimes takes a while to emerge, so I'll give you an example that will show what I mean. Many years ago one of the first people I worked with was Kenny Wightman, a convict locked in the most secure wing of the most secure jail in Massachusetts. He told me he wanted to write his life story because he'd already sold the screen rights to his life and he wanted to be able to produce a book that would tell the real story, not just the Hollywood version. I liked him and what he had to say. I checked out the details. He had in fact sold the rights to his life story to Paramount Pictures, so I agreed to work with him. He was serving a long sentence and needed something to fill his time, to keep his spirits alive, and he hoped the money would be useful to pay his lawyers so he could appeal his conviction. Behind that, though, I sensed a real desire within him to try to come to terms with the life that had led him to where he was at that moment.

We met each week in the grey-walled former death chamber (the remains of the electric chair hookup were still visible on the wall) amid the deafening echoes that rumble through bare concrete buildings where guards and inmates routinely yell at each other. Sometimes we had to speak through a steel mesh, but mostly we were allowed to sit at a table. In the course of our time together Kenny began to see that the more we talked, and the more he wrote, the less his story looked like a simple action-adventure movie. The events were startling, of course, with fast car chases, escapes, life on the run - but we could both see he was beginning to be more thoughtful about them. He was reassessing his life, which seemed oddly fitting in the death-chamber. He was making himself anew as he saw who he had been, and why, and why it wasn't necessary to remain as that other person. "Sometimes," he'd say, "when I look back it's as if I've lived a whole other lifetime, and all this happened to another person." In being able to stand outside his personal experience he could see his actions and judge his life from a different perspective.

And often he wasn't particularly pleased by what he saw. He was, in this way, rehabilitating himself by writing his story. Each day he was saving his soul, one paragraph at a time.

And it worked. He is now a free man again, living a decent, honest and deeply compassionate life. The whole process was very moving for me, too. Kenny had been famous, in his way, for two things: stealing fast cars and daring the police to catch him (they almost never did, much to their fury); and second, he was an inspired, relentless, resourceful escaper. As a youth his entire attitude had been 'can't catch me'. Now he wanted to catch himself so he wouldn't have to keep running. And as he wrote he became aware of something else as well – if he could understand how he had gone so far astray he felt he might be able to use his story to prevent others from following a similar path. When he saw that, he saw that the story was not merely about himself, but it was a story that reached out to others. It transcended him.

That's what writing one's life story can do. It can do it for all of us, even if our lives do not seem at first sight to have been as dramatic as Kenny's. Not all of us have to find ourselves locked away in a hellish place, as Kenny was, before we start to reflect on who we are. I'd have to say, though, that for some people it's *only* when they find themselves at rock bottom with nowhere left to go that they raise the strength to ask, 'How did I get *here?*'

If you've been to rock bottom, in despair, you'll know all about this. And if you haven't been to that point you'll still have met with situations that have caused you to think about how you've chosen to run your life. In doing that you'll be taking on the soul work that is so important if any of us hope to grow beyond being passive victims of whatever circumstances we have blundered our ways into. That's when you will begin to reassess your life story.

The important point is that your life story needs to be expressed in more than just talk at the dinner table if you are to learn from it at the deepest, most productive level. It has to include writing. Michael Herr, whose memoir of his experiences as a reporter during the Vietnam war became his book *Dispatches*, puts it like this: in the book he records that he was going back to the US and before he left he was sharing a few moments with other reporters who had been through similar near-death adventures, wondering how he could possibly make sense of them. His friend Flynn offered him one piece of advice that Herr called "a kind of blessing", and said: "Don't piss it all away at cocktail parties." Herr took the hint and created the extraordinary work that is his memoir, where he asks difficult questions about his own fascination with the war, which again and again led him into highly dangerous situations. The deep understanding came as a result of the writing, not the talking.

Talking about our experiences can help us to let them go, but there may be more to be gained from them, which can be diluted and lost if we're not careful. As a counselor I've noticed how people can talk about their lives and, because talk is so rapid and so hard to pin down, the word choices can lead to distortions, to self-justifications, and to little or large lies and evasions. Talk really is cheap – and often even the speaker doesn't value it very much. When we take the time to write this entire process is slowed down, especially if we re-read our own words, and we can look at what we've written and say: *Is that really the way it happened? Or is that just what I'd like it to have been? How about if I tried to see it from the other person's point of view?* Only writing can consistently allow us that degree of self-awareness. Anyone who's ever kept a diary will know the experience of looking back over the pages and being surprised at some of the thoughts recorded there. Did I really think that way? Well, yes. I must have. Here it is in my own words! And then that recognition leads to another assessment and we move a step closer to a more complex, contradictory version of the truth and away from the self-serving evasions we all like to tell ourselves.

The point is that simply writing things down, journaling or venting, is never enough. It is perhaps no more useful than yelling one's frustrations into the wind and then forgetting them. It works in the short term but in the long term it means the real stuff of experience, upon which wisdom is built, has been lost. If we are to do the all-important soul work we'll need some better tools than just a journal, no matter how diligently kept. We'll need some techniques we can trust. That's what this book is all about. In it you'll find specifically tailored exercises and prompts that will lead you to where you need to go – even if you don't quite know where that place is yet. You'll find techniques for recruiting your Unconscious awareness so that it works for you, rather than against you. As you do so, you'll change your relationship to your own past self and in the process create a new version of you. The pain that you felt will not go away, but it will change so that it no longer hurts in the same way. It will be transmuted so that you stand outside it and do not feel damaged or unable or afraid; instead, if you allow it to, the place where you have been hurt will become your place of strength. What does this mean? Anyone who has been victimized and faced the horrible feelings of that event with clarity will know, in his or her soul, what courage truly is, and will never want to be victimized again. When such people speak out they become inspirations for others, and help them to rise above their own wounds. In this way the world becomes more compassionate and more courageous, one person at a time. In fact it's the only way the world has ever become better.

When you transform your soul and grow in wisdom, you transform other souls around you.

Notes

1. Andrei Tarkovsky's film, *The Sacrifice*, was released by Kino Video, in 2000.
2. Elie Wiesel, writing an endorsement for the back cover of Leon Kahn's *No Time to Mourn; The True story of a Jewish Partisan Fighter*, Ronsdale Press, 2004
3. Michael Herr, *Dispatches*, Vintage, 1980, p.267.
4. An interesting piece of information comes from Joseph Campbell's lectures on Navajo myths, as recorded in *Mythos I*, (Joseph Campbell Foundation, 1996). The legend of the son of the sun and the son of the moon has the brothers go on a quest to find their father, whereupon they are able to return to the world and kill the dragons that have been terrorizing their mother. Once they have killed them, however, the brothers are exhausted and near death. They then meet 'Talking God' who tells them that the only way to recover is to create a ceremony in which they themselves provide their life story as the subject of the dance. As an example of the re-vitalizing power of memoir it is unrivaled. It could also be seen with equal validity as an endorsement of talk therapy. In each case the individual needs to find out about his or her ancestry to find out who he or she is, and then it's possible to kill the monsters that have over-run the 'homeland'- the experiences of childhood. Finally, the psychic work is completed *only* by telling the tale. Telling the story saves the person's life, but only if it is told, or danced, to others and valued in a ceremony, which in turn energizes the listeners. We do not do anything similar in our present day society, and Campbell hints that we are spiritually poorer for that.

Chapter Two

Listening to Your Life: Starting the Writing

So let's begin. First of all, congratulations are in order. You've bought – or borrowed, or perhaps you have even stolen – this book and that demonstrates that you've decided to take the idea of writing your life story seriously. You've made the most important step, and without that step nothing much can ever hope to happen. In getting hold of this book you've told yourself, even if you haven't told anyone else yet, that you feel you have a story that you need to tell, and that you want to do it in writing. You are responding to the prompting that comes from deep within all writers. I've never found a satisfactory word to describe what it is, but it's almost as if the experiences you have lived through or encountered have reached a point at which they seem to want to make their own way into the world. Sometimes when I work with writers I listen to the way they try to describe that feeling of needing to write, and perhaps the best thing I can say to you is: this is your story telling you how it needs to be told. So, be prepared to listen to what it asks of you. Whether you have several hundred pages of writing ready, or none at all, the process will be essentially the same.

Frederick Buechner calls this process "listening to your life" and it's hard to overstate the importance of that word 'listening'. So many people want to shape their information before they've even looked at it fully. Writers regularly come to see me with hardly a word written but a strong sense of how their memoir's chapters will be arranged. It's natural to think like that and it can be a good starting point. But it's actually not always that helpful. Thinking that way is a bit like doing what we all do when we seek to justify our own position after an argument we've just had. We're very likely to want to force the facts into our version of how right we are. "There I was, just minding my own business, when suddenly...." That may be a true statement and it might just be the voice of the injured ego, defensive, looking for pity and seeking an ally. We frequently have to be on guard against this aspect of ourselves, since we're not always right, not always the innocent party, no matter how much we'd like to be vindicated. Being 'right' is a concept that comes from the head, from our thinking self. It's a cognitive defense that makes us feel better temporarily about whatever has hurt us. Real writing comes from the heart and sometimes it surprises us. When the heart speaks we may find ourselves suddenly feeling compassion for those we thought we loathed. We might find ourselves recognizing how insufferable we were at times, how we antagonized others, how we provoked their anger, and how downright mistaken we were. That's what happens when one listens to the story that emerges. It gives us insights and surprises we might not always welcome, at least at first.

You can observe this with children: Freddy pokes at Maisie, and Maisie gets annoyed and hits Freddie, whereupon Freddie yells, 'She hit me! I wasn't doing anything and she hit me!' Perhaps Freddie's actions didn't merit the thwack he received, but he was hardly an innocent party. If we were able to ask Freddie why he did what he did, he might perhaps eventually reveal that he doesn't like Maisie, or he envies her, or he thinks she's spoiled, or he thinks girls are silly. Any number of reasons may exist, all of which have to do with Freddie's sense of the world as being not to his liking. Of course, Freddie probably can't articulate that, since he's only a child and doesn't have the skills yet. In the meantime, though, he'll do almost anything so that he can feel he's right, even if no one else agrees, so he sits and pouts and he's no closer to any real understanding.

We're all a bit like Freddie.

I'll give another example that may help, here. I was speeding down the highway to the bedside of a sick relative whom I feared would die before I got there, when a state trooper pulled me over. I tried to explain what I was doing, roaring through the night on my mission of urgency. Surely he'd see how right this was! Instead he gave me a ticket for doing 80 miles per hour (130 km/h). I drove on, at a more moderate pace. As I did so I began to recognize that I had, in fact, been going much too fast, at night, on a very dark road. I had been foolish and I had been dangerous to myself and to others, and he could have slapped me for doing well over eighty because even though I wasn't looking at the speedometer in my rush I'm pretty sure I was doing ninety. He had in fact been kind, if I'd had the wit to notice it. He might even have saved me from an accident. And when I arrived at my destination my relative was stable and in no immediate danger – although he did die some months afterwards, having never recovered fully. Looking back on that event now, I can see that part of me enjoyed the drama and reveled in an excuse to drive fast while feeling self-important. My attitude was all ego and the trooper reminded me, in his way, of my posturing. It wasn't a cheap lesson, but I paid the fine and wrote a letter of thanks to the trooper. It seemed only fair.

Sometimes when we feel we're absolutely *right* we're not really right at all.

These sorts of surprises await us and can only emerge if we're prepared to let go of our defenses. Here's another example. A man in one of my groups was writing about an uncle who had been unhappy and sometimes violent. He was able to see, as he waited for the memories to surface in his awareness, that he was more similar to this uncle than he had wanted to acknowledge. Realizing this he began to come to terms with his own anger, see where it came from, and start to let it go. He thought he was standing outside his uncle's experience, assessing it coolly. In fact he was facing himself and it was uncomfortable to have to do that. It would have been much easier, and much more evasive, to focus on the uncle.

In another instance, a woman in one of my workshops started her life-writing expecting to produce a memoir about how her brother-in-law had driven another relative to despair and suicide. By listening to her story as it emerged gradually over time, by questioning what she'd written, she was obliged to recognize that other circumstances might have had a role in the relative's despair and death too, since he'd been to some extent isolated from the family. She would read aloud to the group and stop, sometimes, in mid sentence, saying things like, "It can't have been like that, can it?" If she hadn't written her story and then chosen to read it to others, she might never have reached the point of questioning her own words in this way – and so she couldn't have reached the deeper truths that waited for her. What was remarkable was that she tripped up over her own words, her own version of reality, only when she had to read them aloud. There is something in us that will do this. Our reading will stumble when we aren't clear about the truth, and it'll stagger when we tell untruths. It's as if the body knows and lets us feel it, even when the mind would prefer not to be aware. Obviously this was not a comfortable situation for this woman to have to recognize and cope with. Yet seeing things in this new way allowed her to assess the past afresh, to achieve a sense of peace, eventually, that was based more in truth and less in a fixed idea about others and how much they were to blame. Hers is an extreme example perhaps, but not uncommon. All the writers I've worked with, for any period of time, have found themselves surprised in this way, ambushed by the truth.

Not all truths are accessible, unfortunately. One woman who chose to write her life story wanted to present the facts surrounding her husband's suicide, some thirty years earlier, partly because she wanted her children to know what had happened and partly because she couldn't understand the event herself. Obviously, the one person who could possibly shed new light on the event was now dead, and so she found herself writing about all the contradictions in her dead husband's actions. In the end she accepted that there could be no real 'answer', no closure that would sew things up neatly. There were only questions. And in the writing she learned, gradually, to let those questions simply exist so that they did not haunt her or make her feel guilty. It was as if writing, even when inconclusive, freed her. This is a major point. Sometimes telling one's story the best one can, even if there are huge gaps, sends a message to the Unconscious that says, in effect, that the teller has been honest in the face of one of life's mysteries, and that is sufficient.

This is important because what happens during memoir writing is that change occurs in the individual's Unconscious even when the person concerned can't actually describe that change. The same thing can sometimes happen with dreams. Simply telling one's dreams to another can sometimes cause inner blockages to dissolve. One may not be able to analyze them in any meaningful way, and ultimately it doesn't always matter very much if one can. Change still occurs. It's as if the language of the Unconscious, which is symbolic and exists at a pre-verbal level, can be acknowledged as meaningful even though the meaning isn't made plain in the conscious world. This shouldn't surprise us. Anyone who has been moved to tears by music, or by dance, will have a certain amount of difficulty putting into words why the tears welled up when they did; yet something has been communicated at an emotional level that just might be vital. This is soul work happening.

I have a rather hokey comparison I use to describe this phenomenon, but it may help: the Unconscious doesn't need to have everything explained in order to heal us. It's a little like what happens when you take your car to an honest mechanic. You tell the mechanic what you think is wrong, he looks at it, fixes it, and even if he tells you what he had to do, unless you truly understand cars you still might not have the faintest idea what he actually did. But you get in your car gratefully and drive away. You don't really need his explanation, although you do need his expertise. If you had spent the entire day following him around the garage asking questions you would only have slowed up the process and annoyed him. The wisdom of the Unconscious is a little like that. We have to trust it to do what it needs to do. The Unconscious is never dishonest. It's about the most honest part of you, if you trust it. And sometimes we have to go back and tell it to try again because we've not allowed it to be honest with us. Our pride or our fear has got in the way. That's sometimes why we need to rewrite things a couple of times and try them out by reading them to others.

William Faulkner describes this best. There is a memorable passage in *Go Down Moses* in which Isaac McCaslin is trying to explain why he feels he can't accept his inheritance, and he fumbles for words to put his gut feeling into a form that can be understood:

> 'Let me talk now. I'm trying to explain to the head of my family something which I have got to do which I don't quite understand myself, not in justification of it but to explain it if I can.'

Faulkner shows a man attempting to explain why he cannot accept riches he believes to be tainted because accepting them would go against the very spirit of the land he loves, and he shows that attempt as being unsuccessful as communication. The head of his family doesn't truly understand. One might say that part of what Faulkner shows is a man trying to do soul work when he hasn't the resources to explain it successfully, but he goes ahead and does it anyway.

In my workshops I've noticed many occasions when writers have read a piece – perhaps a piece that hardly seems dramatic at first – and then have said, "Phew! I didn't think I'd have the courage to write that, let alone to read it." The release of tension in such instances is remarkable for the individual. There will be smiles, tears, and often the body posture changes to something far more open, much less tense. So what was going on? In brief, the soul was being allowed space that it hadn't been allowed before.

Let's return to the book you are holding in your hands right now. A second thing you can congratulate yourself on is that in getting hold of this book you've made another important step; you have acknowledged that writing may involve getting some guidance and a few pointers. Of course, there are plenty of people out there who will give you guidance, but some of these people know almost nothing about what it means to write honestly about one's life at a deep level. Writing coaches will help you to create a script that, perhaps, you can sell to a publisher. They may want you to conform to 'what the market needs' or to work a specific angle. The result may be good or bad, but I can guarantee you that if you are looking to do authentic soul work, then that is a dangerous route to go. James Frey's famous pseudo-memoir *A Million Little Pieces* may have made him wealthy and turned him into a household name, but I doubt that his manipulations of fact and distortions of reality led him personally to a place of deep understanding or compassion. Still, that was his choice, and he certainly isn't the only person to have turned out a bogus memoir. He created a book that was *entertainment*, but in doing that it was not truly *exploration*. We won't be taking that route. You have chosen to take your project seriously and you've come to the right place.

When I speak about memoir therefore, please realize that I am not about to guarantee you best-seller status on the *New York Times* non-fiction list. No one can predict that. What I can offer you is a coherent step-by-step series of activities and reflection points that will be of real help to you as you write about your life. These have been structured in a way that will take you where you need to go. I've worked now for several years at the Blue Hills Writing Institute at Curry College and much of the material you will find in this book has come out of that program. The exercises and writing prompts have all been road-tested, so to speak, and found to be highly effective. At Blue Hills we've seen how well the program can work. Clearly this won't be quite the same experience as being in a class, yet it can offer you many advantages, since not everyone can travel long distances to attend a weeklong workshop.

So let's get started on some writing right now. You perhaps already have a number of chapters in your files, but for now our emphasis will not be on what you've already written, but on getting the creative juices flowing again. This may well help you to see what you've already written in a new way.

Find a picture of yourself as a small child, preferably less than eight years old and if you have one taken when you were about four or five years old, this would be particularly useful. If you have several pictures from this time look at them all and focus on just one or two. What do you see? Who was that child? Do you remember anything about that day? Do you recall anything about the picture? Pictures of yourself at different ages will be exceptionally useful as you write your life story, but for now we want to focus on this specific time period.

Take some time now to write down your thoughts about that child who was you. Allow ten minutes. Don't do anything else, and try to avoid getting up and walking around. Be with that picture and your thoughts. Now, read through what you wrote. Add more thoughts if you need to. Often the best insights come as a result of adding to what has already been written.

Responses to this exercise have invariably been extremely productive. A young man in one class showed a picture of himself with his two younger brothers, outside their somewhat ramshackle house in Ecuador, and connected immediately with his memories of the poverty he had been born into, the need to guide and be in charge of his younger siblings, and his anger at his absent father. As the young man grew up to become a police officer who was particularly gifted in working with impoverished inner city youth, one might say that the picture he had selected reflected both his pain, and what he had done with his experience of his pain. He'd taken his anger and used it productively, becoming an officer of the law in order to protect those who were now as at risk as he and his brothers had been years before. The picture reflected his strengths and it also reflected the present struggle he had balancing his job, which he loved, with the needs of his own children. The photograph could have been a symbol of his whole life up until that point. This young policeman wrote about all this and then added a significant fact; in the line of duty he'd recently had to use his weapon on a young man who had threatened his life. In what must have been a shattering event this policeman had been placed in a position in which he had to reassess all he believed in - empathy, caring, and trust – and he'd had to shoot to save his own life. This was a major turning point in his life, a source of some grief and pain. By writing about the child he saw in the photograph he was able to connect with his past, with the idealism he had chosen to live by, and to see that his life choices were deep, firmly rooted, and a coherent part of who he was. Nothing could undo the shock of the recent confrontation, but recognizing who he was in his core made it possible for him to continue his work.

He hadn't intended to write about all that when he'd selected the picture, but one might say his Unconscious had made the selection for him so that he could write about what he most needed to express. And here I would like to point out how wise the Unconscious is: it had led him to write about his present suffering, which he would rather have avoided. Yet in the process it also showed him the way to reconnect with what was essentially the strongest part of himself, the boy who knew what he had to do, and knew he had the strength he needed. The confession therefore was not merely a way to wallow in self-pity and pain – it also provided a way to heal himself.

The wisdom of the Unconscious works in unusual ways if we listen to our lives. Here's what another workshop participant wrote:

> Yesterday for example I started out to write one thing for class and a completely different story presented itself! It's interesting. I'm still not sure where this is headed but I am grateful and relieved, really, that the words are coming out and that the job is getting done. (Jane P.)

Notice how the writer is 'grateful and relieved', and yet she knows that whatever it is she needs to write, 'the job is getting done'. If we listen to our Unconscious and respect its promptings, it will help us in just this way.

Another response to this exercise was from an older woman who remembered precisely when her photograph had been taken, at age 4, and how she'd been dressed in special clothes by her grandparents, instructed to sit still, and been given a teddy bear to hold. She described how tightly the child in the picture held the bear, because this was a toy she wasn't usually allowed to play with. It was kept out of her reach on a high shelf and was only given to the boys, since little girls were supposed to play only with dolls in her family. Her overwhelming sense was of the sexism of the household, the controlling grip her grandparents kept on things, and the way they insisted that everyone should look good for the camera, no matter what the reality was. Writing about this picture she could recall her mood at the time and her deep resentments, which had remained for the rest of her life. She even recalled the photographer – a man from the local drugstore who took photographs as a sideline for a very modest fee. This was the social history behind the picture, a picture that said 'this is how we want to be seen'. It spurred her forward to write on a series of memories about her childhood, all of which were extremely revealing to her, all of which explored the gap between what the adults wanted to try and commemorate and what actually was the case.

In those memories, as she looked at the picture she was reminded about just how strong-willed she must have already been as a child of four and how clearly she saw what she didn't agree with. She connected with the event, with the tensions behind the event, and with her own strengths. She saw that in her family the girls were looked down upon and how this had led to some life decisions later in which she did not fully value herself. The picture had revealed to her a major life theme – not being valued – and yet, knowing in her core that she was worthy of respect. In a sense her whole life had been centered around that tension.

I could give multiple examples, but I think you can see the way this can go. Again and again I've witnessed writers recognize some part of themselves in these photographs, and often it has been a part that has been strong – a part with which they needed to reconnect. "You see," said one woman, "I knew even then that there was something out of whack with my family. And I spent years trying to pretend there wasn't." It may be, of course, that some writers project their later awareness onto those earlier images, but on the whole that does not seem to make much difference; one reaches truths that *feel* true, and how one gets there is less important than that one does.

So look at that picture and ask yourself what's reflected back at you. Keep it where you can see it and refer back to it. It's waiting, and it'll speak to you over time, revealing more and more – if you let it. What were your strengths even at that age? If you don't know, now would be a good time to find out. The strengths we start with early in life sometimes go underground, but they're waiting for you to invite them out.

Another exercise may help you here. Take a moment and try and remember what messages you received from your family about who you were. In this case around the age of eight is a good time period so please focus on that. By 'messages' I mean the things that were implied as well as stated outright. For example, who got the new clothes, and who got the hand-me-downs? What does that convey about who was important in the family? Who was expected to do what? Were chores equally divided? Who got punished and who escaped? Who was in charge, and who wasn't? Jot down the things you heard. Perhaps you were told that you were always to have properly shined shoes in public. If so, then that is what you need to write down. When you have a list of such 'messages' you can go back and write more about them. For now, though, we want to gather the messages, and as many as possible. Allow ten minutes for this exercise, and use more time if you need it. This exercise can work particularly well when two or more people compare results. This sometimes sparks new insights.

Thinking about these 'messages' can be very useful because we are, to some extent at least, what we believe about what other people say we are, and how they treat us. Here's an example from a woman whose sister was a big influence in her life. In their home the two girls were told, "Sally's the pretty one, and Jessie's the smart one". And so they went out and lived that version of themselves, relying on those attributes to succeed. The 'smart' one worked at her books and didn't bother too much with expensive clothes. The 'pretty' one became more extroverting. The irony was, as you may have guessed, that they were both smart and both were beautiful, but neither of them tended to believe this; instead they accepted the family orthodoxy about who they were.

Another example was the young woman, the oldest girl in the family, who was told she was the responsible one, and it was up to her to keep her siblings in order and do what the older boys needed. This may have been a convenient role for her parents to force upon her since her mother needed the help with a large family, yet she wrote many pages about how that early imprinting had led her throughout her life to defer to men unnecessarily and to feel she had to organize and direct those who were younger and female. This did not always go over well in the workplace, and in her romantic life it had been a disaster.

The point here is not just to get you writing about your childhood. The point is to ask you to reassess your past in terms of how it has made you, to some extent, the person you are now. It then leads us to consider if this is the only version of who you are, of who you could be. Perhaps there are qualities in you that are waiting to come forward but you never felt there was any space or opportunity. If we are to discover our souls we must be aware of what we did and of the things we were prevented from doing.

So very often we take in the messages the world sends us and we believe them – and they might not be true. We construct a self that says we can't do something even though we've only ever tried it once. Ask any man at a party who 'doesn't dance' and you'll see exactly what I mean. Any man in that position is protecting himself from possible ridicule that may come from others, and we can all understand that impulse. Yet dancing is a primary form of self-expression. It seems a pity to give it up because of what others may, or may not, think of us. Soul work means challenging those tidy boxes that everyone seems so eager to push us into. It means seeing who we became, and seeing that we could have become someone else, also, and that somewhere between the two is the actuality of who we are.

What you write in response to these two exercises may well lead to a longer piece of writing. Keep it in mind. It could well be the start of your eventual Memoir.

Writing like this is a first step towards breaking down the "mind-forg'd manacles" that William Blake described us creating for ourselves. Soul work demands we get out of that jail, and soon. Those 'messages' you wrote down can be like prison sentences that never expire. Seen this way these two exercises together will tell you two vitally important things that you may wish to use in your memoir. First, they tell you where your pain stems from. That's what we've seen in the examples. Later pain may be difficult, too, but that first encounter with the disappointing and unjust nature of the world will be very deep and will have shaped your life. Second, and perhaps more important, is that these two exercises will tell you where your strength comes from. The sense of anger, of 'this isn't fair!' that we've seen in some of the responses is a reflection of the basic inner strength and integrity of children as young as three or four. This is the innate strength you can call on, no matter what happened in the rest of your life. It's always been there, and it never went away.

In workshops people have frequently said these exercises were inspiring and empowering. I'd go further. I think they help each person who does them to reclaim the inner strength he or she had thought was gone forever. Know your pain, and you'll know your strength.

We'll be using writing exercises like this throughout the book. Please, take time to do them, then read the suggestions I make as to how you may be able to view the results, and then write a little more. In my experience in workshops the initial exercises give rise to more thoughts and more writing. If you have more thoughts than you can deal with presently then jot down some reminders for another day. With any luck you'll have more than enough material so that you can't actually get all you want to write completed right away. That's fine. Many of the emotions and memories will wait for you. For now do not worry about where this writing will fit into the whole of your life story. We'll be addressing that later.

Notes

1. Frederick Buechner, *Listening to Your Life,* HarperOne, 1992.
2. William Faulkner, *Go Down Moses,* Random House/Vintage 1973, p.288.
3. James Frey, *A Million Little Pieces,* Doubleday Anchor, 2005.
4. William Blake, 'mind forg'd manacles' appears in his poem 'London', which has been widely reprinted.

Chapter Three

Making Space for Your Writing in Your Life

Now that you've got some writing underway and can see what sorts of things can happen, let's take a moment to outline what we'll be doing here and what is expected of you. If the exercises have worked so far they'll have helped to generate new material. Now we have to take the next step.

I will ask you to do three things:

(1) Make time every day to write, preferably at the same time of day. I'd suggest a minimum of fifteen minutes. Even if you don't write anything at all on some occasions, stay at the desk for those fifteen minutes every day and try and do that four or five days a week. Since I'll also be giving you a series of writing prompts and questions you should find it possible to write a few words each time in response to the assignments. So if you find yourself at your desk feeling blank and uninspired, try the writing prompts on pages 35-41.

(2) Give yourself the space to write. Take this demand seriously. You'll need enough elbow room at a table or desk so that you can be comfortable and feel that the space is truly yours at least while you write. This is hard to achieve if you take your laptop on the train and are surrounded by commuters, some of whom will try to read over your shoulder. Do yourself a favor and carve out some space for yourself.

(3) Relax. That's easily said, but a few basic guidelines may be helpful. Don't sit down to write if you know your front door bell will be ringing in the next few minutes, or if you're waiting for something or someone. You will simply feel rushed. Don't try to cram the time in when you know that the kids need to be picked up in five minutes or the dinner is about to need attention. You can do that if you have to, of course - for example when you get an idea you want to record that's too good to risk losing - but don't substitute that for the real time you spend at your desk. Give yourself this clear space and claim it as inviolable.

So let's look at these requirements one at a time. If you understand the reasons behind them you'll be more likely to use them.

Writing pretty much every day, like exercising regularly, is important. As a rough guide, when you are in the flow you can expect to produce about 250 words a day in an hour spent at your desk. Some days may produce more, much more; others may yield less. But a page a day is a good goal to aim for. You cannot do this, however, if you don't take the trouble to make sure that you write on a regular basis. You wouldn't expect to run a marathon without being in training first. Neither should you expect to be able to sit down and write for hours on end without first getting into a rhythm of practicing. So – choose a time and a place and make sure you stick to your arrangement. Sometimes I've had writers tell me that they have broken up their writing time into two chunks of ten minutes, because that was the length of time they got for coffee breaks or cigarette breaks. Whatever it is you have to do is up to you. But do it. Make the arrangements. If you don't schedule a space in your life for your writing I guarantee that you will not get around to doing it. It's as basic as that.

People are all different, but on the whole it's not a good idea to put aside time at the end of a day as your designated writing time. For one thing, you'll be tired. Of course, you can write a diary that way. In fact if you're recording the events of a day then last thing at night is probably the best way to get it all down because you'll surely forget some important material once you've had a few hours of sleep. The 'Brain Dump' at the end of the day can be very useful and will usually ensure an unbroken night's sleep since you'll let go of the events of the previous 24 hours. But for life writing this will be only a first step. Life writing will need to be nurtured differently.

Most writers have reported that a regular time to write has been highly beneficial. As we settle into a rhythm of daily writing, the Unconscious has a tendency to get itself ready, knowing that the writing time is approaching, and so when the opportunity arrives the words are literally waiting to pour out and onto the page. It's the same sort of thing that happens when our Unconscious is trained to expect meals at certain times. We turn up for lunch, and we may not even be feeling particularly hungry sometimes – but the moment we sit down with the food in front of us the Unconscious brings on the appetite. Sometimes this works to our disadvantage, however, when we find ourselves eating out of habit rather than need, and the extra pounds begin to add up. That's the downside of the Unconscious. But for our purposes we want to utilize the positive power it can provide us with. If you turn up to write at roughly the same time, in the same place, with the same book or laptop or binder, then your Unconscious will be triggered to release all the thoughts and ideas you've been storing up for the previous 24 hours. You'll find you've been 'writing' in your mind all that time, processing material, making connections. The Unconscious is tremendously helpful in this way. It can be trained – and it can be adaptable – but it sometimes takes a few days to get into its preferred patterns or rhythm. Ask anyone who's ever suffered from jet lag and who doesn't know when to eat or sleep for several days after arriving on the other side of the world - a prime example of being off one's rhythm. If you train your Unconscious in this way by turning up at the desk, or keyboard, or table, on a regular basis, your Unconscious mind will work for you and you will get into a rhythm of writing. And just as your appetite comes out of nowhere at meal times, so your writing will appear when the pen is poised.

To do this properly you do, once again, have to listen to yourself and your internal rhythms. Choose a time of day when you feel at your best. So if you routinely feel drowsy at about 3pm, then that might not be the best time for you to try writing. Many people find first thing in the morning to be a particularly productive time – before the cares of the day have had a chance to make a claim on one's mind. Whatever time you choose, make sure that it is your choice and that it works for you.

Sonia Sanchez, in her splendid short prose poem called *Just Don't Never Give Up on Love* describes a semi-autobiographical moment when she's in the park, writing. "I opened my book and began to write. They were coming again, those words insistent as his hands had been … demanding their time and place. I relaxed as my hand moved across the paper like one possessed." It's a beautiful and unnerving piece of writing, and it describes exactly what can happen when you find your groove, your real sense of writing. It can seem to happen through you rather than being something you 'do'. Just as a world class athlete will walk onto the sports field and feel ready to excel, so will you feel ready to write when you claim your time and space. But I have to tell you that an athlete strolling through a scruffy bit of some stranger's back garden will not feel the same way as she will when walking into the arena. Why? Because the mind triggers the athlete relies upon, the sense of the place, the event, the ritual, will not be present, and so she will not even be thinking about performing. This is why it's necessary for you to set aside time, a place, and mental space for your writing. You don't see athletes yakking on their cell phones before a race, or at halftime during a big game. They're at work, doing what they do. And that's the sort of attention to the task you'll need as well.

Giving yourself this time and space is not always easy. Sometimes this will mean rearranging your day. You may have to get up half an hour earlier. You may have to give up that twenty minutes you spend reading the sports section each morning. You may have to skip your daytime soaps. You may even have to cut back the amount of time you spend looking at eBay, or perhaps arrange to pay for an after school program for your children. Whatever it takes, you must do this if you are to be effective in this work. You'll find a way, but you have to take this seriously. That's why we have the next task.

Write a Contract for yourself, in which you agree, in writing, to do these three things - and any other agreements you feel to be necessary for your personal process, such as not getting distracted by the TV, not going shopping for that elusive pair of shoes that might just be in the store now, and so on. Remember, you are agreeing to the three items we've discussed.

First: to write regularly, for a set amount of time;

Second: to make available the necessary physical space to do the writing;

Third: you undertake to do so in a way that allows you to feel unflustered, unpressured, and relaxed.

The fourth thing you will agree to do in your Contract is this: you are to give yourself a reward every day you complete your writing goal, and you must take that reward. So, if you fulfilled your writing quotient and you promised yourself a chocolate truffle as a reward, you *must* take the reward and take the time to enjoy it. No excuses. Take your reward, and only your reward. This is not an excuse to devour the whole packet of candy. This is a treat. Some of my writers have given themselves rewards that are delayed in their effect, but just as useful. One decided to reward herself by putting a dollar into a jar each time she completed her daily writing, and then to reward herself with a massage when she had accumulated the necessary $30. Delayed gratification is good – but please make sure that the delay is not so far away as to seem impossible. Saving for a trip to China at the rate of a quarter a day may turn out to feel like an impossible marathon, and you will be tempted to give up writing; so do what feels good for you. Remember, this is all about you feeling good about your writing and the writing process. If you don't feel good you won't do it at all. If you don't feel validated you'll stop. A small treat, every day, will keep your Unconscious working for you.

Take some time, now, to write down some ideas for your Contract. Have some fun – you can use pseudo-legal language if you want. Once you've written it, keep a copy nearby. Tack it to the wall by your computer if you wish. You can even give a copy to a family member as a way to persuade him or her to understand what you're doing; and you are more than welcome to tape one to your fridge as a reminder and a source of pride. Please note: this Contract is important. If you can't make this promise to yourself, and write it down for others to see, you may want to re-think your motivation for this whole activity of life writing.

Contracts can be long or short, but the longer ones are sometimes more convincing to the writer. The ultra brief: "I agree to write thirty minutes each day" set off alarm bells in my mind when it was handed to me – and correctly so, as it turned out. I was afraid that it showed little real forethought, that it was really too vague to feel real to the writer. Meanwhile the Contracts I have received from other writers have specified things like this: "I agree to write every day except Saturdays (my day off and non-negotiable) and days when I'm traveling. I aim to write 250 words each time." When writers factor in such things as work, travel, known future obligations, and so on, then it is a sure sign they have a realistic grasp of what will be involved and what they must work around. One woman even incorporated a section in which she specified what she would do and what she needed her husband to do. Then she got him to sign it as well. This was, I feel, a thoroughly sensible move, since it's astounding how many men seem to resent their spouse's writing, when they feel the correct wifely thing to do should be to give up the writing time and do whatever the man needs. Including the husband's pledge in the Contract indicated to me that here was a woman who knew what the challenges were going to be and so she had planned ahead. This is sensible. If you cannot plan ahead realistically it's going to be difficult for you to stick to your plan and make the writing projects you undertake workable. So the Contract can help you to plan, to think, and to commit. We all exist in the real world, and the Contract can help us to spell out how we are going to balance the demands it makes on us. That's what contracts are for in the real world – so that everyone knows what's expected and no one should sign one if it's just not workable.

One of my favorite examples of the Contract was one written in a workshop in which the writer included the following:

> Failure to comply with the conditions of this contract more than once in a month during the terms of this contract shall lead to a Visit With The Teacher to ferret out the causes for such reluctance and loss of perspective and in general to resupply the undersigned author with the nourishment required to complete the contract. (Vivian B.)

This particularly amused me since it acknowledged there would be the occasional hiccup along the way. Better yet was that the hiccup was defined, and a stratagem devised to prevent it becoming a problem. So often writers will miss a couple of days, thinking it's not a big deal, and then allow themselves to miss a week, and shrug it off as a temporary thing, until they wake up a month later and can't recall why they stopped in the first place. This is a sure way to let time slip out of your hands. And it's also extremely important to address this right away; real opportunities fade because when we stop writing there is usually a very good reason. The surface reason may be entirely plausible; a visit by the family, a vacation trip, or the crunch of a business deadline. Behind these, though, may lurk other reasons that have to do with us not wanting to write about something we find difficult – so we don't. Yet it is precisely those things that seem difficult that demand to be looked at! A writing block is exactly that – a block that stops you going *where you want and need to go*. If it didn't it wouldn't be a block. Acknowledging a blockage right away allows for it to be dealt with and overcome, and for the riches to be accessed that inevitably lie on the other side of the block. Of course, it may not be possible to break through the block right away ; it may take time and you may need to write about something else for a while. But it should never be ignored. The thing that we are most reluctant to explore is likely to be the thing that we are defending ourselves from having to face. The Unconscious (which wishes to speak the truth), can get hijacked by the pre-conscious mind (which may be afraid of bringing up old events). This pre-conscious mind exists uneasily somewhere between the conscious self and the Unconscious and, since it wants only to avoid any real disturbance, it can be pretty evasive when it wants to be.

So, the woman who spent several months not writing about her father turned out, in fact, to be harboring tremendous anger at him – anger that had certainly helped to worsen the symptoms of her arthritic condition. Since she was only in her twenties and her arthritis was a major part of her life, one doesn't have to think too hard to see that the temptation to stop writing must have been very great. The arthritis was located in her legs and in her hands, strangely enough, which made typing difficult. Isn't it interesting how the body sometimes has a poetry of illness that is all its own – one that seems to point the way to the emotional problems involved? She couldn't go anywhere, in a physical sense, and also in the sense of doing the soul work she needed to do because she couldn't write. Even more interesting to me was that when she began writing, she overcame her arthritic symptoms; today she has been free of them for several years. She told me she also managed to explore her anger through various types of writing until she reached a more peaceful place. I cannot claim a direct correlation here ; I can only observe what happened and say that in my opinion her emotional block actually was helping to cripple her writing hands, trying to silence her - until she decided to go ahead anyway and express her feelings. Releasing the emotions allowed her to reclaim her life and her health. Now she's 'going places' professionally, and also physically, as she is once again able to travel for business. And she writes regularly, too.

This shouldn't surprise us. Anxiety can make any condition worse and can precipitate conditions that would otherwise never arise. One of the biggest killers in the US today, as we all know, is heart disease and anxiety is a key contributing factor to heart health. When we understand our lives, when we do the necessary soul work, we can come to a place of greater peace, and physical ailments will very often vanish.

Returning to the writing Contract for a moment, it's worth giving a few more examples to show how one can approach this in an inventive way. One woman created a law firm in the name of her two beloved dogs, and had them 'sign' the page complete with ink impressions of their paws and a seal provided by her local library's book stamp. And what could be more enforcing than the devoted eyes of two dogs? One could say that she enlisted the blessing and support of two creatures who loved her unconditionally, and who would also remind her that she had to go out and play sometimes. Humor like this is always a good, healthy sign. The woman, who agreed to write "a minimum of six days (not to exceed seven days) a week," showed a keen sense of what she knew she would have to do.

Another example began this way:

> This contract is between Vivian and the compliant half of herself.... It is further noticed that whereas Vivian's rebellious half, Little Vivian, chose not to sign this contract on the date it was written, a line is provided for her should she change her mind. Her compliance would be warmly appreciated.

Beyond the humor lay an important realization. In writing about her childhood Vivian recognized that she'd have to deal with her child self, and that this child self was not always going to be happy about uncovering the events that had been so frightening at the time. This was the part of her that she knew would try to sabotage the entire process, since this child self had to be wrestled with, cajoled and won over. In writing the Contract she had identified one of the central struggles in the writing as well as having named the main struggle in her life. Her life writing would be about healing that rift so that she could be whole. Coming to terms with Little Vivian was an urgent life task as well as a writing task.

So now you should have most of the important things in place that will help you to focus on your writing. I'd simply like to add that since we'll be venturing into some new territory you might want to travel lightly; focus on what practical arrangements work, rather than on what would be perfect. Occasionally writers have decided that they simply cannot begin until they have completely redecorated their 'writing room', or that they have to find a studio away from home in which to write, or that they need a new computer before they can begin… and so on. These are delightful considerations; and you will not do any writing while you are thinking this way. If you find yourself obsessing in this way (and which of us isn't just a little obsessive?) remind yourself that the energy would be better spent doing the writing. You can choose to spend three weeks searching for the perfect notebook if you wish. I don't recommend it, though. It will be a way of avoiding the work that you know is waiting for you, so you may as well admit it and get past it. That may sound brutally honest, but since this memoir will be about saying candidly what your story is, we cannot start being truthful too soon in this process.

Notes

1. Sonia Sanchez, *Just Don't Never Give Up on Love*, *Callalloo*, Maryland, Johns Hopkins Univ. Press, 1984, no.20, pp.83-5. Widely reprinted.

Chapter Four

Establishing a Writing Practice

Now you have a writing Contract, a place that you can claim as your own during the designated time that you're writing, and also a reward to look forward to. Make sure that you honor all these things. A place to write need be no more elaborate than a corner of a table that you claim for your half hour a day, or a favorite chair you can curl up in with your laptop or notebook. But do try to keep all these factors, these coordinates, in place. And if that means shooing the cat out of your favorite chair or ignoring the phone, then that's just what you have to do. This is your workspace. Clearing the decks may be necessary. One person I worked with put it simply: she said, "When I do this I consider myself to be at work. My task is to do this, to write, and interruptions are to be ignored. I wouldn't take a personal phone call at work unless I was on a break or something like that." The message you send yourself is that this is honorable work. Your Unconscious will respond positively.

If all this sounds more regimented than you are used to, I'll point out that getting into a writing rhythm and staying in it will produce more meaningful writing than might otherwise happen. Over the years I have had writers appear before me with sheaves of papers, sometimes more than they could easily carry, that they'd been chipping away at on and off for decades. While this can be valuable material it will more likely turn out to be writing that has recorded surface events and not the meanings behind them. The reason is often that the events have been written down at odd moments, now and then, with no opportunity to dig deep or to make links, and so the deep processes of writing and thinking have not been engaged fully. The conscious mind has been at work, but not necessarily the wisdom that can be accessed by the Unconscious. Since all real change happens in the Unconscious we may find that those four hundred page binders are excellent reporting, but not about in-depth understanding.

So here is my disclaimer. All suggestions I make here are only suggestions. You do not have to follow anything I say. This is, after all, your life story. I will merely point out that if you follow these directions you are likely to save yourself a lot of time and effort and get deeper into the material much more quickly. Ultimately you will find this more satisfying and you will know, every day, that you are doing something that feels useful and that will bring you to a place of greater understanding. Obviously this may call for a few unconventional tactics, at least at first. Some of my suggestions may seem odd. Try them anyway. Often the value of a particular procedure cannot be gauged until afterwards when one sees where it has led.

Remember, though, that I am not trying to force you to be something you are not; whichever way you prefer to write is the one you should stick to. Writers can be very choosy about how they write, and I believe we should respect that. Many people I've worked with have had favorite notebooks, of a specific size, shape or design. This has felt important to them. A friend of mine swears by writing on public transportation, or in public places. That doesn't work for me, but I note that coffee bars everywhere are filled with folks who seem to be doing the same thing. Personally, at one point I found it very helpful to handwrite my drafts on the unused side of scrap computer paper. To some extent it removed the terror of the blank, new, pristine, unmarked page. Somehow I found it consoling to see my own handwriting rather than typescript. Later I realized that what I was doing in choosing to write this way was that I was sending a message to my conscious self saying that this was just me writing ideas on scrap paper; this wasn't real writing, so there was no need to get too anxious about it, was there? No need to start censoring myself. Reassured by this, my conscious defenses switched off and I found I could write whatever I felt I needed to. And so I wrote, and my inner doubts were deflected because this was being written on scrap paper, so it couldn't be important, could it? I was no longer blocked when I wrote in this way. Instead I felt comfortable.

Being comfortable in this way truly matters, and I'd urge you to stay with whatever method you find most congenial. And I also would like to offer you a few ideas for how you might do things a little differently, notions that you can try out and perhaps introduce into your work.

If you write by hand I'd urge you to consider writing using alternate pages, or at least leaving some white space around your words. This is because I will be asking you, as you look at your completed pages, not to revise but to add. You'll be more likely to add to what you have written if there's actual space on the paper so that you can. My experience has been that when we have only a small amount of space in which to write we tend to cram our thoughts accordingly into the space available, and that means we risk losing a lot of good ideas and even important detail. I can guarantee that as you write each day more thoughts and memories will come to you, and you will want to be able to invite them in. So leave some space for them on the page. Throughout the first part of this book I'll be insisting on generating more writing and on adding to it if you wish. We won't be editing for some time yet.

Most people I've worked with write directly onto their laptops or computers, and if this is your method I'd ask you to allow for plenty of white space around your words for exactly the same reason, because I'm going to ask you to print out what you write. I know that may sound illogical. After all, why bother? Why sacrifice all those trees and all that ink? I suggest this because when you print out a page, and it becomes a physical object, you will see it differently. You will notice typos, for example, that you hadn't seen before. That's because to some extent we see what we want to see, and that becomes much more likely when we're looking at a computer screen. But we're not looking for typos now, we're looking to see if we left anything important out. I've often been humbled by the difference between what I thought I had written at the computer and the reality of the printed word on the page. When you have your printed pages, with plenty of white space around the words, then you can re-read and add in the ideas that occur, the memories that suddenly resurface. Notice I'm just asking you to add. Do not re-write or edit. There will be a time for this, but that time is not now. There will be a time, later, when you can refine the gold you have mined, but for now you're still at the stage of excavating the seam, and that is a specific type of work that is very different from what the goldsmith does when he makes jewelry. Editing now will only cause you to inhibit your task of generating more words. Editing at this point will only invite the internal critic in, and it will cause you to be blocked as a writer.

In addition, when you're writing, no matter how you do it, it's always a good idea to keep a spare notebook at hand. What you'll find is that as you're writing away, or as you're contemplating the next paragraph, a thought will pop into your mind that has nothing to do with the work. It'll tell you to pick up the dry cleaning, to call your Mom, that you forgot to pick up milk, and so on. Above all, don't give in to these thoughts or you'll never get any writing done. When such thoughts arise simply jot them down in the notebook. By doing this you acknowledge that this is a task you need to do (because a notebook is a serious thing, unlike scrap paper), and that you aren't trying to ignore it. Ignoring it usually means that it'll come back every five minutes to torture you, often saying things like, 'You promised you'd call your Mom. What kind of person are you, putting it off? I bet you'll forget again, and she'll be waiting, probably, and getting worried. I know you, you always do this....' This kind of internal voice can destroy your progress as a writer, since you'll be constantly leaving your desk to do its bidding, or giving in to its blackmailing ways. Instead you can jot down the demands and carry on writing. Later, when you're done writing for the day, by all means follow up on this list of duties.

This process of invasive thoughts also has to do with the Unconscious mind. Putting it simply, the thinking part of the conscious mind does not really want you to write your memoir because it is afraid of the upset to its routine that may result. The conscious mind tends to be afraid of emotion, and afraid of altering the way things are. By writing your memoir you are threatening the relative stability that it has long fought to maintain, the 'this is the way things always are' mindset that you are currently exploring, challenging, and discarding. And so it tries to sabotage your writing by sending you thoughts that will deflect your attention. For most writers it succeeds, only too well. At times like this I sometimes think of the conscious mind as the bureaucrat, stuck behind his desk, who knows a million ways to delay, defer, delegate, and prevent change from ever happening. That bureaucrat knows precisely how to seem helpful and then will send you in the wrong direction. So by using your notebook and jotting down your list, you will send a message that, no, you are not abandoning your duties; and then you can get on with the writing. To use another simile, it's like lobbing a piece of steak to the guard dog while you slip inside the gates.

If you keep this notebook at your side when you write what you'll find is that after a while your fearful bureaucrat/guard dog will relax, convinced that all is well, and as this happens the thoughts that bubble up will tend to be useful memories you'd truly like to explore rather than errands you have to run. Don't let those new memories deflect you from your writing, either. If you're in the midst of writing about your brother, and a really good memory surfaces about your aunt, then jot down a few words in the notebook, and return to them only after you've finished what you're doing right now. It'll wait for you. Some theorists consider such emerging memories to be yet another way the mind attempts to derail your writing, and they may be right. Our concern here is less with what precisely the mind is doing than with how to work most effectively with what it will tend to do to you.

When you have generated your pages, keep them safe. Some people print them out and put them in a three-ring file; some place them in a box; some people paste them into larger notebooks. My colleague Robert Atwan, who edits the *Best American Essays* series, swears by creating what he calls a Writer's Album into which he pastes everything. I suggest a three-ring file, so that you can keep things readily available but not loose. Loose papers tend to feel far less organized than a three-ring file. Loose papers get lost or crumpled more easily. Again, we are seeking to send an important message to ourselves, here. We're reassuring the Unconscious that progress is being made each time we glance at the collection of script we've produced and note, with satisfaction, how much of it there is. This in turn allows the Unconscious mind to keep cooperating with this task, since you're clearly winning. Better yet is that you will be more likely to be protective of your writing in this form. You'll keep it where you know you can find it. Your project will *feel* orderly, to some extent, because you know where it is. Many writers, I have noticed, feel strangely dislocated from files that are saved on a computer. They can't remember if they actually wrote about an event or just intended to. They don't know where chapter three is, or the episode with the Navajo Indians. Or they transfer chapters from one computer to another and files evaporate, or turn into Japanese script, or go on vacation to Mars. Or the computer dies and they have no back up. I cannot begin to tell you how often this has happened to writers I have known and worked with. As a good friend in the software business says, "There are two kinds of people in the world; those who have had a computer disaster, and those who are about to." And that was said by someone in the business! So by all means save your work to disk, to cyberspace, to mozy.com, or to an automatic back-up device, and please, please, consider an actual, physical file you can place your hand on. It is astoundingly reassuring, I promise you. And if you are to be a productive writer, reassurance will be necessary. Work *with* your Unconscious whenever possible, rather than against it.

Many writers learn this the hard way. The man who had his three hundred pages of script on disk was deeply troubled when he discovered that he'd worked on the task for so long that all the operating systems he had used were now obsolete. The information was on the disk, but he had no way of reading it anymore.

Another possibility to stimulate your writing is what I call the Writer's Shelf. I call it this because in my life it is an actual shelf on which I place physical objects connected with the writing I'm doing, in a place I can see them everyday. Some people prefer, when they hear about how effective this is, to use a shoebox in which to place things, and for that reason I sometimes call this the Treasure Chest. Into it you can place letters, photographs, mementos, dried flowers of sentimental significance, favorite pens and pencils, and so on. Some people have even included old bus tickets, maps, pages torn from guidebooks, concert ticket stubs, and the list goes on. The Treasure Chest is for anything that will spur your memory without letting it drift off into the ozone of idealization.

Having these physical objects at hand will certainly spark your writing. They will also keep you focused on the all-important details of the actual events. If you have any doubts about this just remember that James Joyce, in his masterful novel *Ulysses*, worked with frequent reference to a street map of Dublin, the city in which the entire novel takes place. And this wasn't just because he was living in Italy at the time. He once told an interviewer that if Dublin were to be removed from the face of the earth that very day he was confident it could be recreated using the information contained in his book. The claim was somewhat tongue-in-cheek of course, yet behind it lies his absolute sense of fidelity to actual, observed experiences in the city he had known and loved for so long. The physical world's details will keep us honest, focused on the actuality of what is. For, after all, which of us hasn't altered a memory without realizing it? At any family reunion there will be at least two versions of an event recalled by those who were actually in it. Who said what first and who did what next…. These are things our memory re-invents as it needs to. In the battle between memory and psychological need, memory nearly always loses. Having physical objects to hand will help to redress the imbalance.

The Treasure Chest is not for notes that you want to use to remind yourself of events. Those belong in the text, and you need to take time to add them in, or to write them out as events to be picked up as daily writing tasks. The Chest is for your primary sources, the actual physical reminders of what was. Photographs and press cuttings can be very useful, since they present the material as it was at that time and not as it is now, smoothed and embellished by memory. The great advantage of the Chest is that it can remind us of the double focus necessary in memoir writing. We have to be able to recreate the events as they were, and yet see them with the wisdom that comes from time and distance. So, if you are relating an event that goes back to when you were ten years old and afraid of the Math teacher, you'll have to recreate the moment as it felt then, yet not give in to the memory. At that age you probably just wanted to run away and hide. You didn't have the language to express what was going on. Now, writing the story, you have to face the event and show convincingly what the fear was without making it trivial – because it wasn't trivial at the time! The heart of real life-writing exists in this double focus.

Go ahead and use the items in your Treasure Chest or on your Writer's Shelf. Just as money locked away in a bank vault is not doing very much good, neither will the items you have amassed be much help unless you use them to spark memories. Pull them out from time to time and let them work for you. You may astonish yourself at what appears, asking to be written about. But it can only happen if you have an open mind, and even then it may take time.

My own Chest is actually a shelf of treasured objects, and on it is a tiny photograph of my father at his air gunnery and navigation school in 1941. Fading to sepia at the edges, it has some creases and marks. It was, I think, a picture owned by my grandmother until she died and then my father put it on his own dresser. In it my father is in the absolute center of the group, the tallest, and smiling with real pleasure, the wind ruffling his always-unruly hair. It wasn't until I really started looking carefully at the picture that I began to ask questions about it. He looked happy because he loved flying, and also because the Battle of Britain the previous summer had raised the prestige of the Royal Air Force; so in early 1941 he felt he was part of a winning team. In the picture he is proud, happy, confident. I believe he kept it on his dresser long after the war was over because it reminded him, later, that all but two of the sixteen people in that picture were killed in action and he himself was shot down and spent four years as a prisoner. The photograph acted as a reminder of two states of mind, of a double focus for him, and by letting it work on me I could see how rich in associations it was for him, how it symbolized the dividing of his life into two phases – and thus who he might have been as my father. As to why the picture is so small, as far as I can tell it was one of the few items that survived when a bomb fell on his parents' home in 1942 while he was far away, incarcerated by the Germans. Small things survived better than large ones, and most of the larger pictures didn't make the grade. When I was completing my late father's memoir – which later was published as the full-length memoir *From Coastal Command to Captivity* - this Treasure Shelf was immensely helpful in keeping me grounded in facts. It can be a wonderful way to focus one's attention on important details, so one can show rather than tell; evoke, rather than explain.

So now you have the resources to help you with the work of writing your life, and you have a file into which you can put your work and the ideas that emerge as you write. You also have a Contract with yourself which is every bit as binding as any contract issued by an agent or publisher. It must be honored. Joseph Campbell suggests that when we create a space such as I'm describing, we are constructing a sacred space, in much the same way as a temple or a church is a place designated for a specific sort of activity. You are creating your writer's study, and you will find it provides you with peace and with the sense of focus you need so that you can take on the soul work you need to do.

A few words of warning: Once your writing starts you'll discover that it jumps in front of you at the oddest times. This is because the Unconscious waits until the conscious mind isn't paying attention, when it isn't editing thoughts before they can take shape, and then begins to bustle forward. It is particularly good at doing this when we drive. Why? Because the conscious mind is following the road and the Unconscious seizes its chance and starts to flood our brains. This can make for very bad driving. So please, I want you all alive, unscarred, and living to incredibly advanced ages. If you need to, buy a tape recorder to speak into as you drive. Some people pick up a cell phone and call their home number when the ideas emerge and they leave themselves messages on their answering devices. I'm not a fan of phoning and driving, having almost been killed on several occasions by people doing just that, so I'm not recommending this tactic for everyone. Please take care. You can always pull over and record your thoughts in safety. My students regularly report that when they're in the flow of writing, the words will surprise them in this way. It's not a fluke, but it can be a gift. Sometimes it's a gift that comes in an unexpected form. One woman found herself with poems popping into her head as she was on her daily run – and she'd never written poems before in her life. At first she had to run home fast and write them down before she lost them, she said. After a few occasions like this she started carrying a pencil stub and paper, and she'd stop her run to get the words down. Her conscious mind was engaged with the rhythm of running, and the Unconscious got right to work for her. As she said on another occasion about a section: "It came to me as I was driving, so I pulled over, and it all just came out of me." Later she recorded that she'd started composing poems the same way. "Poems seem to be writing themselves and I just copy them down," she said, somewhat surprised by the process. Other writers have referred to 'the muse' visiting them, demanding that they write. Whatever we think of this we can see that inspiration will strike us, but only if we provide space for it to happen. Sometimes we don't even know the full value of what we're doing until later; "It's remarkable to me how much I don't know; scary but exciting," said another workshop writer, who found herself dealing with waves of memories she hadn't even known she had.

In addition to all this, you may find that writing your memoir leads you to reassess the people around you. You'll want to ask them questions. You may even change the way you feel about them. Please remember that this is a potential growth point in your relationships with others and that any friction that arises is because you may be seeing with clearer eyes than before and with a clearer gaze than some of them can face. Be gentle with yourself and with them. And be honest.

Always carry a piece of paper and something to write with. Really.

Writing Prompts

On the next few pages you'll find a list of additional writing prompts. These are for you to use when you have no ideas that are more urgent, or if you feel yourself to be in a slump. They will help to ensure that you do some writing every day. Keep all the writing that you do. In this way you will build up a 'bank' of writing that you can return to. As with all good banks, your writing will never lack interest….

The writing prompts truly work. Often when we're not sure what it is we want to write we just need a nudge, and when the pen starts to move across the page, or the fingers across the keyboard, we find ourselves writing about something that may be at a tangent to what we were writing the day before, yet it feels alive and vital all the same. Keep writing. Always go where the energy of writing takes you. Do not, ever, stop work and say 'I'm not interested in that series of ideas today because I'm supposed to focus on only the Important Things in my memoir.' In my experience, whenever this has happened it has been because there is something that needs to be addressed, but you are not quite sure how to capture it so it can be dealt with. So, if this happens, notice it, and then ask what might be on the other side of it.

Often I've found that writing prompts have a way of steering us around to writing about what we need to express, anyway, rather than what we'd like to write about. And they'll keep doing that until we pay attention to what our heart is trying to let us know.

So here are the writing prompts. I haven't placed them in an appendix as most authors usually do, because I know only too well that the majority of readers will ignore anything in an appendix, and I do not want you to ignore these prompts. Even if you only skim through them first time around, put a mark next to the ones you think you could use one day. Then you can come back to them.

» What stories were told by your family about your family? Were there any myths, or legends?

» Can you recall any special toys? Are there events connected with these toys? Did they get lost? Did they have names?

» Can you remember mealtimes? Where did everyone sit? What did you eat?

» Who got to sit where around the TV? Who was in charge of the remote? Or was there a TV in each room, and everyone watched alone?

» "The last time I saw my father…." Write about this, or substitute another person.

» Recall some favorite meals or recipes. What memories are connected with them?

» When were you scared? Who did you go to for comfort? Who do you go to now?

» Remember an achievement. Choose one from childhood, one from adolescence and one from adulthood.

» What are you most proud of? Is it the same thing that other people would connect with you? Perhaps it's something no one else knows about.

» What were the family pets? Were some more important to you than others?

» Can you recall every address at which you lived? Every phone number? Are there any stories connected with this?

» "The year I went to college…"

» Do you have a particular possession you always like to have with you?

» Were there family arguments? What were they? Who argued?

» What is the most unusual thing you have, or had, in your home? How did it get there?

» What do you consider the perfect vacation? Have you ever had one like that?

» It's the middle of the night, and your car has broken down. Who will you call? Why? Do you have any memories of such occasions?

» What do you regret having thrown away or lost?

» What was your first job? What did it teach you?

» Who were the mentors in your life?

» What are the significant anniversaries in your life?

» Describe a relationship. It can be to a person, to a place, to a book, to movies, to alcohol….

» Remember a birthday.

» 'Happy Holidays'. Can you recall any family celebrations or religious occasions?

» What do you want people to remember you for?

» Recall a time when someone deceived you.

» Recall a time when you deceived yourself.

» Describe your first car – or any car you think is important.

» Describe a first love. Or a first kiss. First sexual encounter?

» Who do you trust? Why? Who do you not trust?

» Describe a betrayal.

» Write about an obsession – yours or someone else's.

» Write about a crime.

» Have you had a near death experience?

» Have you ever saved a life?

» Describe a party or a public occasion. Was it a time of happiness or disappointment?

» What movie has touched you most deeply?

» Describe an infatuation.

» Where would you like to live? Why don't you live there?

» Write about money in your life and relationships.

» Recall a wedding.

» Recall a funeral.

» Can you remember the first time you met someone who was to be an important figure in your life?

» When have you had to say goodbye to people?

» Have you ever experienced a paranormal event? ESP? Seen a ghost?

» What brings you joy? With whom do you share it?

» "Lousy job, lousy pay."

» "Great job, lousy pay."

» What are your religious beliefs? How have they shaped your life? Did you choose them?

» Describe a mentor who failed you.

» What are you afraid to write about? What do you feel would be *dangerous* to write about?

» Remember a boss you liked, and one you didn't.

» Recall an encounter with a wild animal.

» 'It was a dark and stormy night…' Describe a time you were in a storm, perhaps in some remote place. What did it feel like?

» What was your favorite food when you were a child? What is it now? Can you recall any times when you did not want to eat the food prepared for you?

» 'Up the stairs was the attic…' What was in this attic? Can you recall?

» Recall a moment of embarrassment. Recall several if you can.

» 'Going down the basement steps was like going down a hole.' Can you think of times you felt anything like this?

» Describe a time when you felt invisible or under-appreciated.

» Consider a moment when someone else got the praise for something you did.

» How about a time when you got praised for something you didn't actually do?

» Consider a time when you got blamed for something that wasn't your fault.

Here are a few more writing prompts that come under 'The History of...' label, an idea that came to me as I looked at photos of myself in an album, and marveled that I had ever looked like that. You can add pictures to anything you write, of course. Most good memoirs do.

» The History of my Wristwatches.

» The History of my Raincoats (or Jackets).

» A Short History of my Eyeglasses.

» A Brief History of my Briefs (or any other underwear for that matter).

» A History of my Commutes to work

» A History of my Vacations.

» A History of my Coffee Makers.

» My Real Resume – A History of what actually went on at those jobs.

» A History of my Pets.

» A History of my Luck.

» A History of my Haircuts.

» If you have a photo album you might want to select pictures of important figures in your life and ask what they were thinking in the pictures you are interested in. Try to work your way into their minds.

> » If you have letters or papers in your Treasure Chest, try looking at the handwriting. What does it tell you about the person?

Now, if you wish to take on an even more searching assignment then I'd urge you to consider these 'triple' prompts;

> » Describe something or some event you'd like to recall.
> » Describe something you can't recall fully.
> » Describe something you don't want to recall.

> » I can't remember…
> » I'd like to remember…
> » I'm afraid to remember….

> » I can never remember…
> » I can never forget….
> » I don't want to forget…

Whenever you write, try to recall specific details of the time and place. What clothes did people wear? What scents and tactile sensations do you recall? You can also do this in reverse, so to speak. It works particularly well for me with food scents. Each one prompts a memory. Try looking at a restaurant menu, for example (you don't have to go in if you don't want to) and see what memories come back to you as you consider the listed dishes. The scent-memory is one of the most basic in the central nervous system, and it is said to be one of the most primal. To many people, certain perfumes or colognes, especially if they were used by ex-spouses, can cause powerful emotions to erupt. Certain smells of the fresh air remind us of specific places. Take a walk in the country, particularly at dusk or dawn or after a shower of rain, and the scents will be strong, evocative, and compelling.

Sight is something we tend to take for granted, but we need to remind ourselves to see certain events again. Try this out with an old photograph, as I suggested in the prompts list. For instance, there's Uncle Bert in his best suit. He looks like Uncle Bert as we always think of him. But then if you start to ask questions about what you see in the picture, and cross-examine his best suit, you may get a slightly different answer. Uncle Bert must have been hot – the sun is shining and the suit looks like heavy black wool. So why is he wearing it? And those shoes look heavy and equally formal. So, what does this tell you about the expression on Uncle Bert's face? I have one family photograph that I didn't fully understand until I realized by looking closely at the details of the formally posed picture that my Grandfather wasn't smiling in happiness; he was smiling because he was as drunk as a fish.

Touch is perhaps even more readily available as a resource to prompt your memory. When we shake hands with people we often get a sense of them physically. And who can forget the vinyl seats of those 1960s and 1970s cars, particularly the Plymouths and Dodges? And what about the smell of the inside of Grandpa's car? You can add that in, too. Was it a smooth-riding car? Or was it a rattletrap with crummy suspension and a tendency to wallow on corners? And what was playing on the radio? That can be very evocative, too.

What you will find is that physical sensations will spur fresh memories and insights. They will reconnect you to the real event more fully than anything else. They will help to keep you grounded and honest.

It is also a good idea to include the occasional mention of actual events in a memoir, not just so the reader can position the story easily in time, but so that you can allow yourself to see the event as it was then, rather than as it might be judged now. To do this you might want to recall things like who won the World Series at the time of the specific memory, or who was president and what world events were going on. This is easy enough to research and it can be eye opening. People dressed differently in the early 1960s compared to the way they thought about style in the late sixties. They were preoccupied with different products, hairstyles, slang, and food. A Big Mac and a coke in 1963 conveyed a different set of values than they do today. Then it was 'the future'; today it's junk food.

This leads to another aspect for you to consider, and I can do no better than to use the words of William Zinsser, in *Writing About Your Life*: "The best memoirs are frozen in a particular time and place and social or historical condition." He hints (pretty strongly) that the memoirist should choose a specific primary point of view, a 'frozen' but coherent memory. This is what you can build on. When you have established that you can always add the second point of view of you-as-the-older-writer when the occasion requires it. But if the memory is to ring true it must be seen as it was then, first of all.

Notes

1. Joseph Campbell's reference to a 'sacred space' in which to work occurs in *The Power of Myth* interviews, PBS with Bill Moyers, tape 5: 'Love and the Goddess,' Mystic Fire Video, Inc., 1988.
2. William Zinsser, *Writing About Your Life*, Da Capo, 2005 (reprint).

Chapter Five

Now I've Done Some Writing, Where Do I Start My Memoir?

If you have a heap of chapters already written, or if you are still just starting, this is going to be a question floating in your mind. Where should I start? After all, aren't beginnings vital?

Beginnings are vital, of course, because otherwise the reader may not get past page one, but as you plan your memoir this is not the only thing to consider when you think about beginnings. Perhaps we should say that it's not really where you begin that matters, it's more a question of *how* you begin. Imagine a famous person looking at her life as a successful gymnast. She decides that in order to understand why she became a gymnast it's necessary to write about her love of watercoloring, her disappointments in third grade with the art teacher, and the move to the Bronx, where she had no friends, which in turn led to…. You get the picture. I promise you that if you choose to explore your life this way you may be doing a good, logical, systematic job but you may also die of boredom in the process. All the real energy will drain away. If you are to begin your memoir and pursue it fully then you'll need to think about it in terms of energy, and about what you feel you want and need to write. What are the moments of your life that fill you with energy – the moments that are bursting to be written? For the gymnast it might be the exhilaration of doing a perfect routine. If she's set alight by that, then that's where she would do best to start.

In some ways this book has already been about exactly that pursuit of energy. The exercises and prompts are there to help you uncover what it is that you have been longing to write. When you produce these sections of writing they will be full of energy. And, as we know, energy creates more energy. It's entirely acceptable to begin in the middle of a moment of your life, perhaps when you were looking for answers. Bruce Chatwin's famous travelogue/memoir was titled *What Am I Doing Here?* It begins with him asking himself this question when he found his travels had landed him in the middle of an African coup, and he was trying to work out why he'd been foolhardy enough to go there in the first place. It was a question about the moment – what on earth was he doing in an African jail? It led also to much larger questions about human nature – what is it that leads some men to travel in great hardship to distant and dangerous places? What do they hope to find? What psychic urge does it seek to placate? Sitting in jail, these were urgent questions.

The rule, if there is such a thing, is that in writing one should always go where the energy is. If you try too soon to be controlled and logical then the life evaporates out of the writing, and when that happens you will stop. In order to do your soul work you have to surrender to this energy. Fiction writers often refer to this when they write about how characters tend to emerge onto the page and hijack an entire story. The energy of the character takes over. The same thing will happen with your memoir, and it will drag you along with it – but only if you decide to stay with the energy. While a fiction writer may be delighted that the unruly character has emerged, you may tend to feel that you've gone off course. You may be embarrassed that you feel drawn to write about some of the things you did. Don't give in to that feeling; roll with what comes. Here's what one of my workshop participants wrote about this:

> I believe this was the point after all, to understand how the hell I got here, like this, with these relationships, these recurring situations in my life. And I think I am writing it down for myself to read. It's very interesting. The other day I had the first experience, I think, (when I could see that it was happening) that the writing took over! I was surprised at what I read at the end of a couple of sentences…. I think it was a little bit scary. But oh so interesting. This week I think my book is about child abuse. I defined it for myself when the writing took over. (Jane P.)

I give this to you, just as it was written to me, so you can see what can happen if we stay with the energy. Failing to roll with the material will lead you to writer's block, in my experience. Being blocked is about expecting something to emerge that doesn't want to put its head forth, because it's not truly authentic. It's a bit like expecting a cat to behave well with visitors. A cat is probably going to do whatever it feels like doing. If you try to make it turn cartwheels it'll just leave. No cartwheels, no cat. In writing, you do best what feels authentic to you. 'Best' may not be the most polished writing, but I guarantee you it will be alive. As novelist Tom Palmer once said, "There are only two types of writing; live writing and dead writing". I think we all know which one we want.

Stay with the energy. And if that means writing about your mother's death first rather than about your childhood, guess what? The emotions are pulling you towards one event, and in all likelihood the secondary events will get folded in to that primary story, one way or another. Writing is, at times, like a house fire. You call the fire service, make sure everyone's out, and grab what you can as fast as you can. You don't stand about trying to decide if there's time to get your grandmother's dining table out onto the deck, or if you should try and get the silver next. The comparison to a fire isn't frivolous. If you've ever been unfortunate enough to be in a fire or flood or some other disaster you will know that you very rapidly decide what's vital. When writing about your life you will have to decide what's essential, too, if only because life is never long enough to allow us to write everything. And that, too, is a form of soul work. Knowing what to focus on and what to discard is a huge step for the psyche.

What should I put in the middle?
Once again, this is a question that will bubble up in any writer's mind – and it is a reasonable question, just like 'Where should I begin?' That, of course, is the problem. This is the rational side of your thinking mind and it wants to know what goes where and when, and it wants to know it right now. Unfortunately, as I've already had cause to point out, listening to this voice too soon can derail your writing. It can force you to make a plan that you may find confining or inadequate. What I suggest is that you address this voice in kind and even sympathetic terms, because, after all, it is part of you. It should not be ignored, however. So talk to it. Tell it that it is asking all the right questions, that you appreciate its caring, and that when the time is right you'll be grateful for its input. But right now you don't need it. Think about this as an on-going dialogue between you and a difficult part of your mind. Think of it as a dialogue between you and a child on a trip. As you drive along the child says 'But where will we stay when we get there?' This is a reasonable question. However, on this trip you don't rightly know where 'there' is yet, and so it's a bit premature to worry about hotels you haven't seen. If your reaction is to turn on the child and yell at her, all you'll get is a sulky kid who will try to make the rest of the trip miserable for both of you and you don't really want that. The comparison is apt because we do this to ourselves – we hear the voice asking the question and we then beat ourselves up for asking it and then for not knowing the answer, just for good measure. If you wish to make this whole memoir writing experience impossibly miserable and self-defeating, then I suggest you take that direction.

A really useful technique for dealing with this voice, which many of my writers have found helpful, is to write a conversation with it. Using your dominant hand (the one you usually write with) ask the voice why it wants to know the answers to questions about the contents of your memoir before you've finished writing. Then, take a pen in your non-dominant hand and write the answer. Repeat the questions, with one hand answering the other, for as long as you need.

What we find is that our 'usual' rational selves tend to be channeled into the usual hand we use for writing. The less expressed, more creative, more anxious part of our brains is accessed just a little more easily when we use the non-dominant hand. Some theorists have tried to explain this by talking about the left brain/right brain contrast. The standard explanation is that the left side of the brain controls the right hand and is more concerned with rational and logical processes, while the left hand is controlled by the right side of the brain, which is creative and imaginative. While this is broadly true it is also a process that is far more complicated than this. Whether you are left handed or right handed this exercise can work well because it seems to slow down the response time (it's hard to write at all with one's non dominant hand) and this change in rhythm seems to give the mind a chance to react in a different way than it usually does. Perhaps it sends a different message to the Unconscious. However we choose to see it, the results can be most interesting.

Writers in my workshops who have tried this exercise, usually in a quiet, non-public space, have found themselves caught up in quite detailed discussions with this unknown part of themselves. Very often writing to this 'voice' reveals that it has some surprising attributes. On several occasions I've had writers report that the voice sounds just like a parent or a grandparent, or even a teacher. Often the voice has expressed a lack of confidence in the writer, and has even expressed fear. It'll sound mean at times, saying things like: *you'll never finish it if you don't have a plan*; *you know you can't write for beans*; *I don't think you should be writing like this for strangers to see* – and so on. These are the sorts of voices that come to the surface.

When this happens you have to be aware that these are the words of adults (usually) who criticized you and tried to control you when you were a child, and that at the time you believed what they said. You applied their thoughts to you and accepted them. You internalized their voices. That's why you can still hear them. What we have to do now is to stop taking their orders and start thinking about why they felt they had to give those directions in the first place. The adult who insisted on having a plan was, in all likelihood, a person who was not comfortable with spontaneous and unplanned events. Perhaps this was a cautious or a frightened person. Perhaps this was a controlling person. Certainly this was a person who valued results rather more than process. Whichever way one looks at it, it is a fascinating insight into this person's fears, fears that you, as a child, were able to create in this figure. If this was a parent then you have just unearthed a truly important piece of information – this person wanted to subdue your creativity because it made him or her feel uncomfortable. In fact, this person's comfort was *more* important to her than your creativity or authenticity. Now that's an interesting influence in your life!

Just similarly the voice that said you couldn't write for beans may have come from a peer or a teacher, and it was not a kind voice. It was the action of someone who wanted to cut you down. That suggests that you were a threat to this person, somehow. Perhaps she or he envied your energy or freedom or happiness. That's up to you to explore. The voice most frequently heard, of course, is the one that says it doesn't think you should write this because strangers may read it. This is the voice of prim family values, usually parental, and it's based in a fear that the adult did not want to seem in any way 'different'. But wait! That's exactly why you're writing now. It's because you feel your life experience has been different, in some significant way.

So let me state again what is happening. You are writing your memoir *because* you know you have things to say that are important that you couldn't express in any other way, and that you couldn't express before. Of course the voices of the past will bubble up and try to silence you!

Examples of voices that have come to the surface over the years are many and varied. For example, there was the woman whose Head Teacher took a dislike to her and yelled at her and victimized her for several years, causing her a paralyzing fear of reading in public that lasted for thirty years, when previously she had won prizes for public speaking. By dialoguing with that voice she was able to understand that the Head had been an angry, tortured alcoholic who was fired a few years later, and that it was his demons he was fighting, not anything she did. She just happened to be in the way. More interesting still was that, even though the whole school and much of the community knew this man was bullying her, no one stepped forward to help. She registered this new information with shock. It was a major insight about the climate she grew up in and the clueless conformity of her parents, who assumed there was something wrong with her, not with the teacher. This insight was the start of some deep soul work and the reclaiming of her artistic voice in its fullness.

One young woman reported that she would routinely write pages and pages on her computer and then delete everything. Often she would do so if she thought someone was coming to see her who might read what she'd produced. She decided that she did this as a way of protecting herself, so she wouldn't have to be 'seen'. Some part of her, a part she didn't fully understand, had told her that this was the wise and proper thing to do. In a way the urge was a true one. By not expressing herself she didn't have to explain anything, and she wasn't at risk of any criticism. These 'voices' - as I have called them - are persuasive because they really do have a reason for urging what they are suggesting: it's just that the message they send doesn't apply any more. You don't need to be protected from those critical people now. If you're doing the two-handed writing, you can thank that part of yourself for caring about you so much, for protecting you so well, and ask it if it would please come back another day, but only when you invite it.

A personal side note may shed more light on this: as my father reached his eighties he developed a puzzling and sometimes annoying trait, which was that he'd give advice about every little thing. He'd give detailed advice about how to drive a trip of a few miles – a trip I'd made regularly over the previous twenty odd years. Rather than get angry with him for assuming I couldn't drive myself across town successfully, I recognized that his advice actually came from a place of love and caring. He truly wanted me to have an easy drive. He also was fearful for me – as he'd aged he'd seen many people drive away and some had died of old age before they'd been able to meet again. Every departure reminded him of all those other partings. His advice-giving came from a place of love, certainly, but it was exactly comparable to those voices so many of us hear when we write, that seem to want us to do things *their* way. As writers we have to learn to accept the voices of advice that we hear as having real power, and yet not give in to them.

To return to the question of what you should put in the middle of your memoir, I can say that the middle of your memoir will be about you uncovering the questions of your existence. It's not so much a case of whether you traveled to Nepal and whom you met there, but it is rather more focused on what it meant for you.

Ah – but perhaps you don't know yet what it meant for you! Write it anyway and then apply the memoir writer's most valuable word, *because*. As you read your work over you will find that much of it doesn't need to be explained with a 'because'. And sometimes it will.

An example I'll give is the wonderful writing one woman produced about her desire to train for a sport she could do following surgery. She elected to be a mountain hiker, and rapidly decided she'd train to climb all the forty-eight 4000 foot (1220 m) and higher peaks in New England. Her descriptions were exquisite, as was the sense of what it felt like to clamber up steep and difficult terrain, and then to scramble down again. Then, several months into the project, she wrote a shorter piece she intended as a magazine article; in that piece she explained that it was the friendships she had developed with her faithful hiking buddies that were so important, as she struggled to regain her sense of personal well-being and empowerment following her surgeries. Getting fit again was her way of refusing to let the illness wear her down, and her friends had been her treasured supporters in this effort. In effect she had written the 'because' piece that answered the question, 'Why are you telling us this?'

It's a necessary question. We read for information, certainly. If I read about a nineteenth century explorer I'll be interested by the information that is preserved in the pages. But we also read for insight and wisdom. If that explorer tells me about human nature, shows me something I hadn't noticed before, I'll be delighted. We write for the same reasons; we record what we feel needs to be recorded, and we find our ways to wisdom, insights, and understanding as we do so.

My own memoir writing has followed a similar pattern. In one section I wrote about my hobby of restoring antique motors of various sorts, and as I did so I was led to think about why I did it, as well as what I felt about the people I had met along the way. I kept asking why we did what we did. The answers were not always flattering. Sometimes it was because we wanted to have something that no one else had, and that's about as selfishly egocentric a reason as anyone could ever admit to. Then I began to notice that most of the people in my hobby had no children, or if they had they were distant from them, and I began to suspect that this hobby was a way of being a child without having to apologize, amongst other things. As I made this and other connections I found myself in a new space, one in which I had to ask whether this hobby was providing me with anything that I needed out of life. Eventually I concluded that it was an activity I had taken on because it helped to disguise from me what I wasn't prepared to explore yet, which had to do with wanting to be recognized and accepted by my father. Since I'd started the hobby at sixteen it had, to some extent, always been about adolescent needs for recognition. I still fiddle with old machinery. But I do it less now. Since I've made some connections about why I do it, I've found I have much less need to do it. This is the strength of those 'because' questions.

You may find that as you write for understanding, and as the understanding arrives, you will give up old patterns of behavior that filled a gap for you. You may regret this, or you may be relieved to know that you don't have to stay in the place of doing an activity simply because it disguises you from yourself. Such activities are a way of feeling a feeling without having to acknowledge the full depth of the emotion. In my own case the machinery restoration was a diversion of just this sort. My friends used to refer to their obsession with this hobby as their 'disease', one that couldn't be 'cured'. Well, it can be cured, because once you know what the compulsion is, you can choose not to be ruled by it. A different example springs to mind of a man in my counseling work who was having trouble giving up smoking. As he said to me after he'd given up the habit, he realized that he'd only taken up smoking as a young man because in his urban neighborhood men standing outside had to be doing something or they'd be regarded with suspicion. Smoking gave him a valid activity then, and now he recognized he didn't have to do it anymore. He'd taken up cigarettes as a way of looking as though he had a purpose, when really he just wanted to get out of the overcrowded house for a few minutes (he had nine brothers and sisters). Now he had his own place and the diversionary activity of smoking didn't serve any purpose.

I don't want you to give up your hobbies, of course. I'm not here to spoil your fun. But I am here to encourage you to take up your true work – soul work – and it's my task to point out that your hobbies and obsessions may just contain valuable clues about what your soul work actually involves. If, like me, your hobby was a way of trying to make contact with your father, or to win approval, then it's a good thing to recognize that and to ask how much of your life is given over to trying to gain approval from people in such indirect ways. There may be a better way. This, too, is soul work.

Notes

1. Bruce Chatwin, *What Am I Doing Here?* Penguin, 1990.
2. Tom Palmer, personal communication.

Chapter Six

Should I Work Alone or with Others?

I suggest that once you have started writing you may want to choose an informal writing partner or two, if you so wish. This is not mandatory. Some people feel they cannot share their writing. If this is your situation then respect it, maintain your privacy, and keep writing. I will point out, though, that the transformative power of life writing is best accessed by sharing what you write. The writing will help you to uncover what you know and what you feel. Sharing it will do something more for you: it will allow you to present parts of your experience to others so that you, as you do so, can stand outside your own experience. As you do this you will discover that others are not shocked by what you say. You will find that your experiences have to some extent been validated by the simple fact of others having heard your words. Sometimes they will hear or read what you have written and be inspired to tell of their own life episodes, and perhaps that too will help to validate your own experiences. It'll almost certainly cause you to remember more. And when this happens more material flows. Stories lead on to stories, and that's true of sharing just as it's true of your private work. Sharing what you have written also allows you to grow your courage. You get used to speaking your truth, so you do it more easily.

In the groups and workshops I've led this sort of sharing can be extraordinarily powerful, both in terms of what it can do for the quality of future writing, and for what it gives back to the soul of the writer. Being able to write about an event like childhood abuse takes courage. Being able to read it aloud becomes a declaration of independence – a far stronger, more empowering statement that says, in effect, I refuse to remain silent about this; and when that happens the others in the group are always moved, always respectful, and they in turn become inspired. It's a process that I've sometimes called 'finding your voice', because at that point the writer is refusing to whisper and begins to live out loud. In real terms, the choked up voice of pain and fear can be transformed into the clear, firm, reading voice that is yours, waiting to emerge, as you tell your story. I've witnessed it too often to doubt it. Hearing oneself read the words of a sad or unpleasant event can feel distressing in the moment, but the pay off will come later. From such actions courage and wisdom grows (for what wisdom can exist without the courage to speak it?) and as it does so the soul of the writer is transformed.

A woman in her forties arrived at my class afraid to say much, and when she did speak it was in a high, child-like voice, which sounded timid and thin. Then, over the course of a couple of weeks, after she read to the class some of the exercise responses she had written, she began to sound different: more of a contralto than anything else.

When we speak out in this way something extremely interesting happens. Whether we're reading a section about being abused or simply about being misunderstood, the same forces are at work. At the time we were being mistreated and we knew it, yet we felt we had to keep quiet because we thought we'd be hurt more if we did manage to speak out. To some extent this put us at war with ourselves, and an action that we longed to complete – to say that we felt mistreated – could not be completed. This sort of experience can find oblique expression in neurosis, or sometimes in physical symptoms, since it can't find release in any other way. So the woman who spoke in the small child-like voice had adopted that mannerism because it felt too dangerous to be fully adult at that time of threat – and at any other time she felt under threat, or uncertain. Speaking out our truth allows us to complete the frozen action, or actions, of so long ago. It is immensely releasing and is the way to let go of pain and resolve previously irreconcilable neuroses.

As you write watch out for this. You will find that writing and sharing your feelings will unknot what has been tense in you for years. Like all releases from pain and discomfort you may not notice it at first, but then that is so often the way with pain that leaves us. We forget we ever had it. The poet George Herbert puts it best in 'The Flower' (1633):

> Pain melts away
> Like snow in May
> As if there were no such cold thing.

So how do you select a writing partner?

If you know someone who is also writing and whose opinion you respect, then this person might be a good choice as a writing partner. I'd strongly caution you against choosing a spouse, significant other, parent, or close relative. I have nothing against these people. I would only observe that when people are close to us, the relationship has in all likelihood gathered a certain amount of history. Our friends may want us to be a certain type of person, and may not be prepared for us to be who we are when we write. Working to complete my father's memoir after his death I received all kinds of well-intentioned advice from family members who wanted this event added, or that, or thought I should write it as a thriller, or as an historical piece, or as if from the point of view of another person. I consider myself fortunate that I listened to none of their advice. If they wanted to write that story then they were welcome to try, and good luck to them. But I had to be true to what I felt needed to be said. I knew I had to tell the story a specific way. I had to honor what my father had written, and I also had to make sure it was accessible to others and not just a private document. I like to think the result was successful. If I'd taken all that well-meant advice, though, the memoir would have been a mess.

Some writers join groups with a leader, and this kind of set up works well. The leader's job is to keep everyone on task, so that things don't degenerate into idle chitchat. The mere presence of a leader is often enough to focus the mind on the task of writing, and to make sure that the meeting has a designated end point as well as a specified starting time. Remember, the saboteur that lurks at the edge of the Unconscious will do almost anything it can to avoid dealing with the difficult material that is in your life, so it's going to give you a lively time as you try to approach your writing – which is work, after all. Our task is to get the Unconscious to work for you, not against you. As we've seen, the Conscious part of the mind likes to be comfortable and will shy away from all possible upsets to that equilibrium, and so it will try to keep the Unconscious from expressing itself. So we need to make sure the Unconscious, which is often full of unruly emotions, is on our side, here. Sometimes I think of the Unconscious as being a bit like a large dog. It'll do whatever it can get away with. But in my experience a truly happy dog is one who knows what is expected, and when. So, when you plan your meetings with your writing buddies, be aware of this so that your time has a structure. Make sure everyone gets equal time. Make sure everyone is respected and respectful. Soon enough, like that well trained dog, your Unconscious will know what's going on and will realize that it's not going to get hurt, and it'll cooperate with you. In case you think I've used the comparison to a well-trained dog at random, I'll just point this out: dogs are extremely sensitive to what their owners are feeling. They know your emotions sometimes before you do yourself. In addition dogs are also totally present in the moment. What matters to them is what is going on right now. As such we could hardly ask for better role models in the realm of the emotions. They witness our emotions and they accept, unquestioningly, what we express.

Dogs need structure – and they love it. So, too, your reading group will need a structure if it is to thrive. Arrange to meet regularly, keep the appointments, and respect the starting time and the ending time. Don't call up and reschedule at the last second. That sends a message to your partner and to your Unconscious that says, 'this is not important.' The most successful writing partners I've observed have put aside a certain time and a certain day every two weeks or so, and kept to it, and they've remained at it for years through several writing projects. They start promptly at a certain time, although they may allow fifteen minutes at the start to get coffee or whatever they need; they scrupulously allow each writer a certain amount of time to read and be responded to, and they keep to that; and they end on time. If this sounds a bit like a committee meeting I'd have to say that, yes, real work gets done. And it can also be a lot of fun.

Writing partners can work in many ways – email, fax, or phone. I like groups to meet personally, although some people like the phone and deal well with Skype or iChat. I find that email is a poor idea – it usually causes misunderstandings at some point, and I think that has to do with the way we read from the computer screen as opposed to the way we hear voice inflections. However you prefer to do things, make a regular time to check in with your writing partner, and keep that appointment. In my extended workshops we find that checking in every two weeks is not a bad way to proceed. Any more than that can feel like pressure – and when we're under pressure we may feel we have to write what is expected of us by the others, rather than holding true to our own writing.

It's a very good idea to read your work aloud to another. Over the years I've found that few things work as well to reveal the strengths and weaknesses in a piece than to read it out loud. As a reader you will stumble over the rocky expressions. That's how you'll know you need to fix them. You'll get confused when your writing isn't clear, and that'll tell you what you have to take care of. You may find that you are very funny when you write – several writers I've worked with have been delighted to discover that their humor count has been far higher than when they're chatting normally. You will certainly find that the poignant parts are more poignant than you had imagined they would be. In classes and workshops I have regularly witnessed writers choking up and even weeping as they read. They usually apologize – which is entirely the wrong way around! If there are no tears for you as you write and read, there will be no tears for the audience. Tears let us know that the writer is working with real, raw, feelings. Without them there will be no memoir worth the paper. Writing your painful experiences, reading them aloud, and hearing your voice as you do so are some of the most powerful things you can do for your psyche. I have taught workshops for twenty years now, predicated around the idea that we all have a voice that is waiting to be heard. Perhaps we've been afraid of what others may think if we actually used that voice, or possibly we've been afraid of the pain we'll cause ourselves. These fears keep us in self-editing mode. Self-silencing would be another way to describe it. It's time to move beyond that. When you read your writing, especially the difficult parts, you'll be empowering yourself to speak your truth, respect your truth, and explore it more. As one woman said to me, "I was so afraid to read [this section] aloud. I thought the world would end if anyone heard me say how I really felt about my mother. I thought I couldn't stand it. I didn't dare. Now I've done it I feel as if I've had eight tons of garbage lifted off my back." (Paula C.)

Reading aloud is good for the soul.

If you do decide to have a writing partner there is only one rule I'd ask you to observe. Focus upon what works in the writing, first and foremost. If a section does not work for you then say so simply, and let the matter go. Do not try to re-write it for the other person. Above all do not tell the person who is reading what he or she should be feeling about an event. Writers feel what they feel. We can always ask questions, but it is not up to anyone to direct another's emotions.

As you do all this please bear in mind our main purpose, which is that we intend to keep moving ahead. So, revisions, line editing and tinkering will tend, actually, to defeat the purpose of what we do and you will quickly bog down if you once get started on this sort of rewriting. Again, I can't order you not to do it; I can only urge you to avoid it as a trap. When the whole memoir is nearing completion we can go back and tidy things up. That is the appropriate time.

Reading with others can take many forms. One woman found that she could get all the benefits she needed by reading to her cat. She was able to read expressively (more expressively than when people were present) and she got to hear her piece and respond to it. The cat, it seems, was very happy to be read to, and it watched her without dozing off or getting distracted. We'll never truly know what the cat thought, but that probably doesn't matter, as he knew he was fulfilling a purpose. Another woman discovered, quite by chance, that when she read from a magazine to her dog that the dog would either be relaxed and attentive or would become agitated. So she wrote down the passages at which the dog became unsettled. What she discovered was that the dog, probably responding to some slight change in tone in her voice, was likely to become uneasy when she read about situations that made her uncomfortable and which referred directly to her life experiences. It was a startling demonstration that our voice has a tendency to alter when we deal with emotionally-laden material and that this change is available for others even though the words may not be.

Reading your work out loud connects you with a powerful source of energy, and it deserves to be tried regularly. In the previous chapter I suggested ways in which our own internal 'voice' can be crushed by others or taken over by the voices of authority. Reading aloud to others you trust, and whom you know will be paying attention, can help you claim back your authentic voice very rapidly.

It's a two-stage process. First you notice what's been stolen from you; then you find a way to get it back.

Notes

1. George Herbert 'The Flower', written in approximately 1633. Widely reprinted.

Chapter Seven

Letting Your Story Tell You How it Needs to be Told. Generating New Material

A t this point your major task is still to generate new material. Now this may come as a bit of a shock to some of you as you may have already accumulated lots of writing, parts of which feel substantially complete. Do not worry; that writing will be useful, so hang onto it and don't start cutting and pasting from it just yet. When you wrote your previous material you almost certainly had a sense of what you wanted to say, in general terms, but probably you did not have a truly coherent sense of how it needed to be said, or how best it should be presented. That's not a criticism; for if you were already sure about what you needed to say and how, then you would probably not have picked up this book in the first place.

So let's look at your work as a series of first steps. You have, as it were, as-sembled the building materials. Now that we have the materials we are ready to design the house, making sure that we fit it properly into the terrain you have to build on. As we do so we may find we need more of certain items, such as nails or wallboard or electrical wire. You may need to fill in the details. And just as a house must have an identifiable front door that leads to a hallway, that in turn will lead to a series of rooms coherently arranged, so your story must be made accessible to all who read it. In a diary you can be as confused as you wish. But this is memoir writing, and part of our aim is to make connections that will be coherent so that you will be able to understand how your life episodes fit together. So, like it or not, we are in the business of shaping what will be a narrative, or a series of narratives. At this point some of you may be delighted that we're finally getting to put some shape to all this writing, and others of you may be feeling that you didn't sign up for something that would lead to the production of an actual narrative, because all you thought you wanted to do was personal writing. This is where I have to tell you that the only essential difference between these actions is what you do with the completed draft. If your life writing is to make sense to you, you will have to proceed as if you were writing to an audience, because ultimately that audience is you. The soul work we are engaged upon can only happen if we bring the information and the understandings into a narrative form that can be understood. Why this has to be the case I cannot easily explain; the only thing I can say is that I've worked with enough writers to be able to claim that unless the narrative that emerges has a logical and coherent pattern, a bit like a memoir, then the writer will not feel the work has been completed and the soul work has not been achieved. So, to all intents and purposes you are writing a memoir at this point, and that involves finding a structure you can work with.

Perhaps a comparison will help. When someone has gone through a difficult time, he or she will attempt to *explain* it to close and trusted friends; whether we're the one talking or the one listening, this is an individual trying to make sense of the events for his or her own benefit. It feels necessary to do this. What we notice at times like this is that the speaker will frequently stop and say things like, 'No, that can't be right' or 'Let me try that again, because that doesn't make sense.' This tells us that we have a need to make sense of our lives, in one way or another, and we don't feel we can stop until we have done so. 'Sense' to most of us, looks like and needs to be a coherent narrative that starts, develops and ends. It needs to be something that someone else will also agree makes 'sense'.

Thinking of this task as being similar to constructing a house may be a helpful metaphor. After all, one lives in a house just as one lives in one's life. So how are you going to set up this house so it makes sense to you, and to any other person who wishes to walk around it? You can, if you so wish, have your front door open up directly into the laundry room, but this will confuse your visitors and they'll never quite recover. It'll confuse you, too. Laundry really isn't the most important thing in most of our lives, so encountering it every day like that can be disorientating. Your visitors will certainly not feel that a trustworthy or sane architect has designed the house. Generating new material is the most reliable way forward if this house is to be all it should be. So often I find writers who agonize over whether chapter three should be after chapter one, or moved to chapter six, and how much back-story may be needed... What they are really doing is endlessly rearranging existing material, trying to make it fit. The cure is to create new material and very often that will answer the problems in a different way. In my work with writers I've found again and again that some questions about the structure of a story just cannot be answered out of the mind set that looks upon already completed 'chapters' as sacrosanct.

The second task is to visualize the narrative arc of your memoir, its trajectory. This trajectory may well change as new and unexpected material emerges and so the two tasks will directly affect each other. Not everything you write will necessarily belong in the full memoir; yet everything you do write will cause you to rethink what the final memoir will involve. Sometimes writing memoir is like going fishing. You know that you'll be eating a fish dinner that night, but just

what fish you'll catch, and which ones you'll keep, you can't accurately predict be-
forehand. Selection is the name of this game, and that's what a memoir involves.
It's always worth recalling that autobiography is the story of a life; memoir is a
story composed from a life. So an autobiography might be the story of General
Sir Alfred Haig's entire life, from babyhood to grave, while a memoir might be
David Kidd's remembrance of just two years he spent in China as it collapsed into
Communism. Memoir tends to select, and so it tends to need shaping.

This is an important distinction. A memoir can be written about oneself or
about another person, and can be a slice of life that is as brief as a few days. Joe
Simpson's story of falling off a peak in the Andes and his miraculous survival
covers a period of just over two days – days in which his companions thought
him dead and in which he struggled with a shattered leg to crawl back to his base
camp. The main impression one gains from this memoir is of a life at a moment
of extreme crisis and self-evaluation. But it's not a long period of time. It gives a
glimpse of one of the central experiences in one man's life, at the end of which one
feels that this is an essential part of knowing who that man is.

Perhaps it will be helpful here to refer back to the time I spent working with
my father on what was to become his memoir *From Coastal Command to Captivity;
The Memoir of a Second World War Airman*. When we first started thinking about
this project he felt he had to write all his reminiscences of almost everything in
his life. He did this and produced three volumes, complete with photographs and
memorabilia. As he did so, however, he knew that much of what he wrote would
not be of interest outside the immediate family. It was only when he focused on
his experiences as an airman in early 1941, which led to him being shot down
and spending the next four years in German prison camps, that he was able to see
the effect of that time in shaping the rest of his life. It was a moment of profound
change, a series of actions that led his life in a completely different direction from
anything he had imagined, and which left an imprint on him that lasted until his
dying day. Writing the memoir became, for him, an ongoing struggle to ascertain
what his life had been about. Its completion brought him to a place of peace – and
the ghosts of nearly sixty years were no longer running his life. He had no idea the
story would lead him to this point when he began. And perhaps that is the single
most important thing about any memoir – each one that's worth reading will take
the reader to a place of hard-earned wisdom, which the writer has felt the need to
try to reach for him or her self.

My father's memoir is not likely to win any prizes any time soon – he was in
an unglamorous part of that enormous conflict, and he was part of a time when
Great Britain was losing more encounters than it was winning. Yet I mention it
here because it seems that the pursuit of understanding, which leads in turn to the

achievement of inner peace, is what propels memoirists to write in the first place even if, like my father, they don't seem to be fully aware of that when they begin. It was in the selecting of a specific time period and series of experiences that he was able to do this.

The important point we need to take away from this as writers is that memoir is about selection, and selection provides emphasis. We aren't really attempting to tell the whole story, even if that were possible. We're selecting because in the end there is a point to what we are saying. This sometimes comes as a surprise to some writers. So let me put it this way: when Russell Baker wrote his memoir, as a seasoned writer and journalist, he set to work and produced four hundred typed pages describing his life. He brought it to his publisher who, after a pause of several weeks, asked him to try again, saying that what Baker had produced was typing, not writing. Baker then went back to his memoir and rethought the whole project. What he realized, as he worked at it, was that the actual story was not the story of his life, but the story of his relationship to his mother. He went ahead and wrote that story and the result, *Growing Up*, rightly won a Pulitzer. It remains one of the great memoirs of our time.

What made the difference between an unprintable, dull script, and the marvellous item we have now, is that he found the real theme of his life, and then wrote about it. Yet it wasn't until he'd written the first version, in full, that he could truly see what his theme might be. That theme also happens to be one that is universal.

That's what we'll be doing – identifying the themes of your life so you can write about them. Whether you call it reframing, or identifying the true story, matters far less than that it happens. If we can do that now then we won't have to write out the whole memoir first, as Russell Baker did.

Here's another exercise that may help you with this, which has to do with creating your projected book's cover.

I'd like you to try this exercise so that you can begin to see your work in a new way. Close your eyes. Imagine that your memoir is published. What does the physical book actually look like? Can you see the title? What is it? What does the cover look like? What color is it? What is the artwork? And when you turn it over you see the words on the back that explain the contents. What do those words say? Are they dramatic, such as, 'The harrowing tale of one man's fight to overcome….'? Or are they calmer? For instance, 'When she revisits the town of her birth the author uncovers the true strength of those she grew up with…' What does your back cover blurb convey?

I'd like you to take some time now to create the cover of your book, complete with the title and the back page write up. This is not an exercise that commits you to anything. You are doing this just for now. You are always free to change the title later on in your writing process. With this in mind think of the back cover. The write up, or 'blurb' should be a hundred words or less, but probably not less than fifty. Have some fun with this. If you wish, find a book of the approximate size you envision your finished book will be, and cover it with plain paper. Then design your cover. Use any colored pencils you like, or anything else, such as paints or stencils.

The great advantage of this exercise is that it allows us to play, while also showing the writer that a real book is a finished product to aim for – something that has solidity, weight, and a certain number of pages. The Unconscious mind registers all this, and its strength is allowed to emerge as you visualize the goal of your writing.

So – what title did you choose?

If you can create a title, or even several titles to choose from, you have made a huge step forward. You have named a major theme or motif that your memoir will explore and you have declared a starting point. In your back cover blurb you will be spelling this out to yourself in ways that you will not be able to ignore. It's a little like finding a thesis for a college term paper. It tells everyone, including yourself, where you are going to begin and what you are going to explore.

This can be a highly effective exercise, as writers who do not have a title are often somewhat unsure about what it is they are trying to convey. This is a way to change that uncertainty. Perhaps you came up with several titles. This is good. And those different titles are likely to be linked in some way, which will be worth exploring. Usually the different titles represent different themes that your book will need to examine. In which case you know what your story is likely to involve, and what it is likely to exclude.

The back cover blurb is likewise a way of focusing. If you can't explain what you feel your memoir is about in a hundred words or less you may need to consider the question more deeply. For your writing will only be as good and coherent as your vision of the whole book. One woman had no trouble at all identifying the main theme, "It's about how to forgive my mother," she said, and in declaring that she knew exactly what one of the main thrusts of her work would have to include. A middle-aged man immediately came up with "Traveling to the Four Corners" as his title, which he explained in his blurb meant the four corners of the USA, which he had ridden to by motorcycle, bumping over dirt roads when the asphalt gave out until he could claim he had indeed ridden to the point where there were no more roads. What had been a series of somewhat random episodes took on, at one blow, the shape of a quest. A different example was that of a woman who declared right away that her story would be about 'Twelve Women' who were the strong women in her life who had guided her when her mother had failed at the task. I could multiply examples but they would all show roughly the same thing

– that finding a provisional title and being able to give it a few, focused, words of description can be a marvelous way to concentrate one's mind on the central issues of the task at hand.

If the exercise has sparked new ideas you may want to take some time and write about that now. If you are bewildered, and have been unable to complete the exercise – which can happen sometimes – don't despair; just return to it in a week or so. Perhaps you could even write about why it didn't work for you as that can often be very useful.

Keep the book cover you create. Place it somewhere you can see it every day. Return to it from time to time and look at the cover. If you wrapped the cover around an existing book, feel its physical presence as you hold it. Place it on a shelf with other books. As you go through the writing process you may need to remind yourself about your story. You may need to rethink certain aspects of it. This cover and blurb will act as the original blueprint, your original rough map. The message you send to your Unconscious will be that this project is happening, it's real, and is going to be completed in one form or another. Remember, this is only an exercise for now. If you want to change your title later you are free to do so. But for now you need a starting point.

Now you've got a starting point, try this exercise. Try to remember the house or home you lived in when you were a child.

If it helps, close your eyes. Think back to the home you lived in at about the age of eight. What can you remember about it? Spend some time trying to recapture it. Now take a piece of paper and draw a floor plan of the home as you recall it. If you make a mistake in the dimensions do not erase it. Leave it in. This may be helpful later. If you wish you can draw a picture of the outside of the house as well, but try to create a floor plan first. Allow about twenty minutes for this, and feel free to write down any thoughts it brings up. When you've finished the plan see if you have any pictures of the house.

Many people have found this exercise to be unusually helpful in prompting them to recall facets of their lives that they'd buried; often it has produced results that they have found illuminating. Perhaps it's unleashed a series of memories already. In which case, don't hesitate – write them. At some point, however, take a look at your floor plan for a second. Do all the rooms fit together? Did you have to re-sketch anything? If so, what was it? Which were the areas you remembered without effort? Where did you include the details of furniture and so on?

The first thing to say about this exercise is that we remember the things that were important to us at the time, and we tend to recall them as bigger than they in fact were. So you might be able to draw your own bedroom accurately, but does it fit in with the rest of the house dimensions? What were the areas you could not recall? Most people will recall the areas of the house that were important, such as the kitchen (where people congregate for food, warmth and company) and the place the TV was. If you needed the refuge of your bedroom, or some other private space, you are likely to draw that place in bold lines, and make it larger than in fact it was in relation to the other parts of the home. On occasions people have reported that they had to draw and redraw the lines to get the plan 'right', since they may have felt that someone else in the family had a bigger room, or controlled more space than anyone else. For this is what this plan can be – it can tell us about the power dynamics within the family. Who got to have the biggest room? Who 'owned' which spaces? Which places were you not allowed to go? Dad's workshop or the best sitting room? Were there any places you were afraid to go?

One man drew his home fairly rapidly but then drew the woodshed with some care, and he explained that he had to run and hide there to escape his father's drunken rages. Another man could not recall where his parents' bedroom was – which caused him to reconsider why his father was always asleep on the couch when he came down each morning. The tale told at the time was that his father had been working late and didn't want to disturb his mother. Yet with the benefit of hindsight he recognized that this time period was directly before his parents' separation, and his father had actually been evicted from the bedroom. Another writer, a woman, couldn't even mention the piano room, although she drew the yard with energy and enthusiasm – and it emerged that she'd been sexually molested by her piano teacher.

Choosing the age of eight is not random, either. At that point in our lives we have many ambitions but we have no power. We want to be astronauts or adventurers, but we can't even set our own bedtimes. We start to have homework as school gets to be serious, and not just a place we meet our friends for play. We can no longer get away with things by pretending we're too young or too ignorant. We may hate green beans, but we have to eat them now. At that age we are simultaneously aware of our desires and not yet powerful enough to do anything about them. So one's house, as recalled, can become a map that reflects the power balances in the family at a time when we were particularly sensitive to such issues. What can you learn from yours? Who had all the power, all the attention? Who dominated the largest portion of the space? It might not be who you thought.

Many writers I've worked with have been moved to recall their homes and have written pieces that were, in effect, walks through the house. A particularly moving piece was one that described the writer being brought home as a new born, being taken in through the front door, up the stairs, placed in the crib, and so on. A different, more disturbing memory was produced by a man who recalled, as a five-year-old child, trembling in horror and fear as he faced an angry, drunk father, who was taking off his belt in order to beat him. In this extraordinarily tense piece of writing he described the father as, for some reason, hesitating and changing his mind. He didn't beat him. The fear and trauma were no less, I suspect, than if he had. But he didn't. And the man was able to see that an event that didn't happen was far more important than some of those that did. He knew that to some extent he'd always been the favored child of the family and that his childhood had been different from all the other children, even though he did not know why. He knew that he'd seen something that day that was both repulsive and yet, in it's own way, loving. The father had managed to wake up to the basic fact that this was a child, and that beating a child was not acceptable. How is it that the man was able to see the child for who he was, and to love him, when he seemed not to be able to love the other children so easily? In this instance it gave a possible starting point for the whole memoir.

The point to ponder is that doing an exercise such as this can lead us to surprising information and insights that we might not have consciously ever been able to access otherwise. Significant memories lurk in odd places.

Another version of this exercise involves comparing photos of the actual place with the memory one has of it. Sometimes this too can be surprising. Even better can be a visit to the place itself. Joan, one of the writers in a class I was giving, recalled that one day she noticed a young woman standing in the road outside her home, gazing at it, and when Joan asked her what she wanted she related a story about how she had grown up in the house and had always wanted to see it again. Joan invited her to look around. Then the young woman asked if she could see the garden. Once there this young person, aged about 24, went and sat on a large boulder, and burst into tears. She sobbed for 45 minutes, then with a faint smile thanked Joan and left. Whatever it was that came back to this young person was assuredly powerful, and could only have been triggered by the experience of the actual place. Several months later Joan received a thank you card from her visitor, and since the younger woman had not remembered her name it was just addressed to 'Mrs. Wonderful.' So, as you do this exercise be prepared for it to surprise you with the hidden emotional content it will release, and cherish the sense of peace it can give after the emotion has been fully felt.

Not all such experiences are quite so pleasing. One man recorded going back to the place of his birth and being greeted with suspicion and disdain by the woman who answered the door. She had no time for him, didn't care about what he was doing, and told him he couldn't take a snapshot. Disappointed, he walked away, only to realize, later, how much he had wanted to idealize this pilgrimage.

The suspicious homeowner had wakened him to his unrealistic hopes and he'd seen the pettiness of the small lives of his hometown in a new light. With the idyll gone, new insights were available.

Many years ago in my work with adolescents there was a similar exercise that was organized for children in the care of the local authorities. The idea was to take them back to all the places they had lived, even the birth hospital, and then take a photo of the adolescent standing in front of the buildings that had been part of their lives. The pictures would then be put in an album, and labeled, and this was sometimes the first step in getting the child to write or talk about things long forgotten or repressed. For children who felt as if they didn't belong anywhere this could be profoundly reassuring, even calming; and it allowed them to move beyond a general feeling of alienation and into a particular sense of what happened during their earliest years. It was, in fact, a map of one aspect of their lives. Knowing where they had come from, even in this basic fashion, allowed them to feel that there were attachments in their lives and that a sense of belonging could exist even for those children who had been through dozens of foster placements. In gathering a sense of their past they were sometimes able to formulate a sense of what their future might one day become.

Behind this lies an important point about memoir: it is always anchored in fact, in detail, and in event. The blanket statements we tend to make about childhood being idyllic or hellish are not helpful to a reader and they're usually not even accurate. It is only when we go back and allow ourselves to see exactly what *was,* that we can come to a true sense of what it might *mean.* That's in part what your writer's Treasure Chest can do for you, if you use it – it can put you back in touch with the physical actuality of life in a way that nothing else can.

The final thing this exercise can show us has to do with structure. Just as a house has rooms, so a story has chapters that must be linked together in a coherent way. And just as we must go in through the front door, walk around the rooms, then exit by the same door, so must we construct our stories in such a way that they take us along in a controlled fashion until at the end we are in the same place as we began, except this time we will have far more understanding about what lies behind the façade. We'll have more to say about this later, but for now you may want to hold the thought as you begin to consider how your memoir may be telling you the way it needs to be shaped.

Notes

1. David Kidd, *Peking Story: The Last days of Old China,* NYRB Classics 2003. (reprint).
2. Joe Simpson, *Touching the Void,* Vintage Classics, 2008.
3. Russell Baker, *Growing Up,* Signet 1992.

Chapter Eight

Understanding the New Material and What it can Give You.

I'd like us to start this chapter by doing an exercise, which I call the three gifts exercise. It's one I've used for years and it usually brings out interesting things. It's a form of visualization, and in it I will lead you through a scene that I would like you to imagine. You can either read the whole scene and then jot down your responses – sometimes one word here and there is enough – or you can read, jot down a word or phrase, read on, and so on. When you come to the end of the exercise you may want to reflect for a moment or two, perhaps to write more about your responses, before you move to the interpretative section. Ideally, if you have the opportunity, get someone to read this aloud to you as you sit back with your eyes closed. If you don't have anyone easily to hand, you can make a recording of the exercise and then play it back when you are able to clear some time for listening and for the writing afterwards.

Sit comfortably and relax. Focus on your breathing for a moment. Take at least four deep breaths, exhaling slowly after each one and if it helps, count to four on each exhalation. Try not to hyperventilate; just breathe in and then breathe out with full awareness.

Now imagine that you have a day off. There's nothing to do, no phone to answer and no computer to check. You decide to take a walk. You can walk anywhere you like. As you walk you feel the air, perhaps you feel the sun, and you look about you. Up ahead in the middle distance you see a figure that looks familiar. You're not sure who it is, so you walk a shade faster, trying to get closer. You still can't work out who this figure is, but whoever it is looks very familiar, so you walk just a little faster. The figure remains ahead of you, and as you begin to get close an obstacle comes between you. Perhaps the person turns a corner, or walks round something. You follow and as you go round the obstacle you see this person face to face. What does this person look like? Do you recognize him or her? Does the person smile? How is this person dressed? Well? Badly? Be detailed here. Then the person begins to speak with you. At a certain point you notice this person has a bag. What sort of bag? In it are several gifts for you. What are they? Describe them. Do you take them all? Perhaps you give some back. Which ones? Then you hear a sound, perhaps a clock strikes the hour, or your cell phone rings and you realize it's time to go. You exchange some parting words with this figure. What are they? Write them down. You walk away. At a certain point you turn around for a second, perhaps to wave. Is the figure still there? What are your feelings at this point?

When you've jotted down your visualization take a moment to reflect further on it. Do the gifts mean anything to you? If so, what? What did the exercise convey to you?

This can be a potent exercise, so you may want to take whatever it is you recorded and consider it with care. Sometimes when writers have done this exercise they've met relatives, some alive, some long dead, and sometimes they've met themselves either as older or younger versions of who they are now. For our purposes I'll point out that whatever you imagined is yours. I gave you the prompts but I did not tell you who to see or how that person would behave. You chose those factors. And so everything you 'saw' came from you, from inside your psyche.

Who you saw, therefore, could mean very different things, but in each case this is the figure in your life that you need to meet in your writing; this is the figure with whom you are going to have to create a relationship. Sometimes people report that they have met grandparents, who remind them of the unconditional love these figures once gave them. Sometimes people meet themselves as older or much younger figures. Sometimes people meet with lost friends, and occasionally with lost tormentors. If you are expecting this figure to give you support and permission to write, then I'd have to point out that this is an emblem – this figure exists in your mind, and the real figure may not be able to give you permission and support any more. Instead of that, something more powerful has happened: your memory of that person has produced an imagined situation which now allows you to accept whatever help you think that person could have offered. That tells us one thing - that you can give that help, that support, that trust, *to yourself,* any time you want. You don't have to wait for someone else to give it. In fact in this visualization you just gave yourself what you need.

Often people will write about being handed pens and notebooks and being told it's alright for them to write what they want to. This is, pretty obviously, people giving themselves permission to write their life story, when their conscious self has doubts about whether it will be 'worth while'. One of the most frequently reported details is that the person has a largish bag, which most people call a messenger bag. It's a tiny detail, yet if this is the case you can regard this bag as containing the 'messages' in symbolic form that you perhaps hope to receive. Sometimes people write about recovering long-lost items. One woman wrote about being given a favorite camera she'd lost in a lake many years before and which had effectively halted her interest in photography. She was, one might say, giving herself back what she needed to keep her creativity alive. I have also seen, on numerous occasions, writers who have visualized their grandparents, who have then assured the writer of their unconditional love and support. Usually the grandparents are long dead, and what I witness is the writer sending herself a message that she deserves love and support and is now giving that to herself – perhaps for the first time for decades.

Not all visualizations are so comforting, however, and sometimes they can even be disturbing at first sight. One woman wrote that she saw two young children with red hair, running through the trees. She knew exactly who they were: they were her two sons who had died in their early teen years. She wrote that she had expected she might see her other child, who had died just a few years before, but instead the two boys from more than a decade ago were the figures who appeared. It was at this point that she recognized that she had never been able to heal properly after their deaths – barely two years apart – and that this was her memory reminding her of the relationships she needed to complete. The focus of her memoir shifted from a sense of general personal tragedy to a more precise awareness of what she had wanted from those sons and how sad she was that they had not lived to deliver on her hopes for a large family of children and grandchildren. In a real sense the figures who appeared represented the relationships she had to heal – in this case her relationship with herself whenever she thought about her dead children. This was the soul work she needed to do so she could make sense of her life. When the figures appeared in her visualization, she said, it was as if they were giving her permission to look at something that had turned to tragedy and instead of focusing on the heartbreak, she was able to recall the love they had shared.

Another woman met herself at aged nine, and couldn't believe how happy that child was. So I asked her to consider what it was that the child could teach her. What was it that child could tell her about being happy? She began to understand that her memoir might have as one of its themes the way we can return to a place of happiness despite what the world throws at us.

The objects that we receive as gifts in this exercise, and sometimes the objects that we give back, all have significance. What is it you are waiting for the world to give you? If you wait for the world to do so, you may be in for a very long wait. Yet if the exercise can tell us anything it is that we can give these things to ourselves. In fact, we just have. So, quite often people relate stories of figures who hand them pens, or completed books, or publisher's contracts, and my answer to that is that we cannot wait for others to provide what we hunger for. This is your Unconscious telling you that you are ready to receive these things, but only if you make them happen. Sometimes the objects can be what I call totemic objects – they have a significance that is specific to the individual's belief structure. So we may see stones - emblems of unbreakable dependability - or perhaps puppies – emblems of love and playfulness – and so on. What is the significance of the objects you were given? On occasion these have even been real, long lost objects that the individual has mourned. In such cases they have always had a story attached: usually one that is deep, rich and complex.

Consider the objects you received. Several times when writers have shared this exercise there have been examples in which they've been given bottles of beer or other alcohol, which they've then, almost always, handed back. The symbolic importance of this is fairly obvious most of the time – it's a handing back of a substance that can really only get in the way of true creativity. Sometimes it has represented the rejection of a whole lifestyle. In each case the message has been profound.

The objects, then, can be seen as symbolic in the deepest sense. The stones that some people receive can be, perhaps, symbols of endurance and solidity, which they feel only someone else can provide; and in great measure that's up to each individual to decide. Just as I may walk in the country and pick up a stone, which I then decide to keep, what it 'means' may be hard to pin down, but by allowing myself to listen to that internal prompting I am likely to be energizing something vital within me. For years I had a small stone that I picked up on a path in Assisi, Italy. I couldn't tell you exactly why I loved it. But it sat on my shelf for a long time, until it got lost in a move. If I'd had my Treasure Chest I could have kept it safe and preserved its peculiar power; but I didn't know about that then.

Once when doing this exercise a young woman reported being given a glowing blue rock by a figure who looked very like her grandfather. She decided to keep it. She had no idea what it might mean and neither did anyone else, but she was happy about it. Some weeks later she shared with the group that she was pregnant and that she must have been only a couple of days pregnant when we did the exercise and she didn't consciously know that she was at the time. She was convinced that the rock was her unborn child. Since she was in her twenties and unmarried this could have been a difficult situation, but her fiancé was supportive and there was never any doubt that she wanted the child. Reflecting on this specific exercise she also said that she felt her grandfather would have approved of her fiancé and that was why he had appeared in the visualization. Months later she contacted the group to tell us that of course the rock was blue – because the baby was going to be a boy! Now, we could dismiss this as coincidence if we wish. Or we could reflect that women sometimes 'know' they are pregnant before the tests ever come back positive. Whatever happened in this case this young woman herself was convinced that this was a message from her Unconscious telling her that her grandfather would have given his blessing to this unplanned event. The visualization gave her the reassurance she needed as the pregnancy went ahead. She gave this gift to herself so that she could move forward with her life. What can we conclude from this? First, that there is a great deal we know that we don't allow ourselves to know; and second, when we do allow ourselves to know our own inner wisdom, it can guide us to where we need to be.

So let's review this for a moment. The questions the exercise can cause us to ask here can be boiled down to some really basic issues. What is the relationship you have to understand or heal so you can write this memoir? That could well be reflected in the person you meet. Are you waiting for that person to give you permission to write? If so, permission was just given, and you gave it to yourself.

Similar questions can be asked about the objects you receive. Are you waiting for someone to give you something so that you can feel complete or whole? If you're waiting for a shadowy figure to give you that best-selling book with your name on the cover, well, guess what? It won't happen. It's up to you to take your own advice (because everything in this exercise came from your imagination, so it's all you) and it's up to you to make sure you claim those gifts from yourself. That means you'll have to take actions to bring this into reality. If these are things you need, make sure you know that your Unconscious just gave them back to you. The lucky stuffed bear, long lost, that one woman imagined receiving was an object that was all about her wishing to feel safe enough to trust her own writing. If she'd been given that precise stuffed bear at that moment it would have been less use to her than the knowledge that her courage was already present, waiting to be expressed.

Whatever it is that comes up for you, it is sure to spark ideas for further writing.

This would be a good moment to try another exercise, one that I've used for many years when working with writers of all kinds. It goes like this: I'd like you to take a new piece of paper and write at the top, "I'm here because…"

Finish the sentence - just a few words will do.

Now, take that newly added half of the sentence and make it the start of the next sentence, adding the word 'because'. When you've done that fill in what comes to you as a result of that 'because'.

An example of this might be:

'I'm here *because* I'm sitting at a desk to write;
I'm sitting at a desk to write *because* I think I have a memoir inside me;
I think I have a memoir inside me *because* I have a story to tell about my father;
I have a story to tell about my father *because* I've never forgiven him…'

And so on.

Take this exercise as far as you can, and if you hit a block, start over.

When you've written a couple of these, consider which of the responses you'd like to write more about, and then write them while the responses are still fresh.

Each of the words of this exercise can be useful. 'Here' after all, can be interpreted many different ways. It can mean where you are physically, or where you feel yourself to be emotionally in the broader sense of your life, or it can also ask the direct question, why are you writing at all? What I have noticed is that writers find this is a way to peel off layers and get to the center of what their life may be about, in general terms. On several occasions I've had writers moved to tears as they've identified that what brought them to here, to this moment, might have been the desire to free themselves from memories and the wish to say what actually happened that particular day long ago, or perhaps the need to convey what changed their lives. As one man wrote, "I'm here to write about those who died because otherwise no one else will be able to do it." Take some time now to write this. Don't rush it.

So, where did you get to in this? Did you come to a personal awareness? If so, then you can be fairly certain that this item will be a theme, if not the major theme, in your memoir. It also honors the most important factor: that all of us are driven to write, to express ourselves, for reasons we haven't fully spelled out even to ourselves. The need to express oneself bubbles up. If you are a painter or a musician, the way this comes into the world, the actual product, will be quite different. For a writer it's about reaching into the barrel to find out what's in the bottom, and what's there may not always be what one at first thought.

This is an exercise that can be repeated successfully many times – especially if you find yourself feeling stuck about what to write next. You can alter it to "I'm writing this because…" or any other variant that serves your purpose. One man even started with, "I can't write about this because…" And at the end of his piece he discovered that none of the reasons for not writing had any real validity in his mind. In fact his responses listed all the people who he thought would be offended if he were to write what he truly felt and why he imagined they would be upset. It provided him with a handy checklist of all those who had been in some way a factor in him censoring himself. His soul work was to recognize that he wasn't concerned with what others might or might not feel; he was doing this for himself. It also provided him with a list of people he'd have to include in his writing if he were to approach the way he'd been silenced by them over the years. To some extent the theme of his memoir became his struggle to move beyond all of them.

As we noted earlier 'because' is a vital word in all writing, and it can be especially useful when pursued in the way we've just explored. It's a good word to be in the habit of using. For instance, sometimes writers will bring me chapters that

are full of interesting events, delightful or dramatic scenes, and yet I have no idea
where the section is taking me. On those occasions the most productive thing to
ask is "I need to know this because…?" 'Because' will supply the missing links, the
connections that you as the writer may not even know yet. That scene with you
watching you father kill rats in the barnyard is important because…?

'Because' can be one of the most valuable words for you to apply to your own
writing.

By now you should have several more ideas about what there is in your story
that needs to be written. Pursue them. It's best if you don't put them off for another day, since the energy that memories and intuitions bring with them can
often be extremely helpful in getting other ideas and memories to surface.

At this point you may find yourself with plenty to say about the story that will
one day become your memoir. Remember: don't go back. You are, at present, here
to generate new material and as you do so you will inevitably see events in entirely
new ways. The temptation is to go back and tidy up the sections you've written,
rephrase, polish and refine. So I'll say it one more time: DON'T DO IT. I can
think of nothing that will kill the writing urge faster or more surely. There will be
a time for going back and revisiting, but that time is not yet. Your writing time
is for writing, only. If you go back it is in order to add but it is an exceptionally
poor idea to go back and line edit. To do so now would be a bit like arranging the
furniture in your home while the workmen are still building the walls. You can do
it if you really want to, but it will be a complete waste of time and will only result
in damage to the furniture. Line editing is a wonderful thing, and you will have
plenty of opportunity for it later.

Under-confident writers fall into this trap like lemmings plunging off Norwe-
gian cliffs at migration time. Those first few pages get honed, refined, rearranged,
agonized over and rewritten until the writer can no longer recall what it was that
was being said in the first place. I've seen it all too often. When I was a student
I used to work in a beautiful circular library. Every day I would take a seat, and
every day I would watch as a man of about 30 would tackle his work. He would
pull a large sheaf of papers out of his briefcase, settle down and every day he
started at page one. I was sitting sufficiently close that each morning I recognized
the same top sheet as the day before, and I would steal covert looks at him as he
wrote, crossed out, rewrote, thought, crossed out, and reworked that opening section. Sometimes he'd get three or four pages into his manuscript before the end of
his working day. Every morning he was back at his seat and back with page one. I
worked in that library on and off for a couple of months and, even at the end of
my time there, when I'd finished my thesis, he was still to be seen going through
his routine, refining the same heavily annotated page one, which was now curling

at the edges. Now, I may be wrong, but I cannot help feeling he was doing exactly the wrong thing if he wanted progress. I learned from him. So can you.

Chapter Nine

Now it's Time to Talk about Structure....

When we talk about structure we're always going to be talking about selecting. So let's start with the most basic structure that exists.

Almost every story has to have a beginning, middle and an end. Without any of these elements readers will tend to feel confused and even short-changed. It seems we are genetically programmed to accept this as an overall structure where narrative is concerned. However, the beginning cannot just be any beginning, or the reader will lose interest. You may not care about the average reader if you are writing this for your family, yet I'd urge you to take the lesson and use it anyway. Consider the average joke. It starts with a premise or situation, it moves to a complication of that situation, and concludes with a resolution. Without the resolution there is no 'pay off' for the joke. Small children in attempting to tell jokes often miss out one or more element, and the result is unsatisfying for all concerned. But a joke rarely starts with a situation that is not compelling. "A man walks into a bar with a green dog...." "Two rabbits walk into a restaurant and the first one says..." Each of these situations is obviously odd and immediately raises a whole series of questions, and you hope it engages the listener enough to stay listening. Notice, the joke teller doesn't bother to explain how it is that rabbits talk or choose to go into restaurants, or why the dog is green. We are landed, pretty much, in the middle of a situation that is already complex, already alive, and which has its own logic.

If we refer to Aristotle, that reliable ancient, we'll see that he has already spelled out the four elements of the drama (which was about the only narrative form most people were acquainted with at the time). He identified these as Situation, Complication, Crisis and Catharsis. The Situation in plays such as *Oedipus Rex* and *Antigone* is already complex and it gets more complex as each new character enters, adding information and contrasting views. We are plunged into the midst of things. When the Complications have piled up and the action seems to reach a point at which nothing can be resolved peacefully we have a Crisis. In it drastic actions are taken. People kill each other or themselves.

Their deaths allow the viewers to see the situation in a new way and the Catharsis occurs because the audience is able to look upon the scene after it's over and draw some human lessons of value. Let's take a specific example, for a moment. In *Antigone* the play starts with a complicated situation. Antigone herself is in an unwinnable situation. She has to bury her dead brother or the gods will be insulted, but if she does so she will be branded as a rebel, since the king, Creon, has forbidden her brother's body any funeral, because he was also a rebel intent on attacking Thebes. It's a splendid case of damned if you do and damned if you don't. Antigone values the gods more highly than the king, so she sets out to get her brother's body. This puts her on a collision course with authority, and it also involves her fiancé, who happens to be Creon's son. Things are certainly getting more complicated. Various people come to try and talk Creon out of his decision, but his pride – and his fear – will not let him bend his will, which complicates things further. Antigone is taken away to be walled up alive in a cell, and this is just about when Creon begins to think of changing his mind, so he goes to her cell, where he finds his son, distraught with grief because Antigone has hanged herself. Enraged he turns on his father and attempts to kill him, before killing himself. Clearly this is a major Crisis. Creon, fleeing back to the safety of his palace, is now left without any heir, whereupon his wife kills herself in grief. We witness and feel the emotional outpourings of three people, each of whom resorts to suicide; one out of deference to the will of the gods, another for love, and the third from grief. What we in the audience learn from all this will depend upon who we are, yet one can be quite sure that amid those lessons are some that refer to duty to the gods and to one's family (even when dead) and how it can conflict with the letter of the law. It has to do with pride opposing love and it certainly examines the nature of loyalty. To have been enabled to see these conflicts may not be the same as solving them – if any solution could exist – and yet it allows the audience to discuss these abstracts in a new way. We are not ancient Greeks, but I think we can all identify with Antigone's struggle as she strives to do what she believes is right in the face of tyranny, even though she knows it will destroy her. That is the nature of Catharsis as we mull over the content of this play. It lets us see things in a broader, more complex view, and it shows us the universality of some types of human situations. And in that process it broadens our minds.

Now, this is a very basic pattern, but highly useful. In your memoir you will certainly have not just one complication, but probably several. Each one will be a moment of some drama and each one will need space. I'd suggest, though, that the overall pattern is worth following.

An exercise will help you here.

Write down twelve moments in your life, which you feel marked a point of change. Just a few words will do. Don't describe them yet. Be aware here that a point of change can be anywhere. One's wedding day is a point of change, yet the decisions that led one to that day may have been rooted elsewhere, and the wedding itself was most likely just the formalization of a series of emotions that were set in motion long before, when you fell in love. Write down more than twelve occasions if you wish.

Now, select six from your list.

Put those six in order of importance. These may well prove to be 'must have' moments in your memoir.

Now, select four. What is the connection between any of those four?

You may discover that your memoir, which you had thought was about how you made a success of a boatyard, is in fact a story of your three closest friends. Now that's a major shift! You may find that your memoir of growing up in a family wracked by alcoholism is, in actuality, the story of the strong women in your life outside your birth family, all of whom helped you to save your own life. The memoir is therefore not about the 'family' but about those outside the family who became more important to you. Sometimes stripping one's life story to its essentials in this way allows us to see the larger patterns that have shaped our lives – patterns we might not have seen otherwise. One man recorded that the four major shifts in his life all occurred in reaction to his parents' wishes, and so he was able to ask himself how much his life had been shaped by rebellions of various sorts. This led, in turn, to the recognition that he'd had frequent and difficult struggles with authority throughout his life. Recognizing this was important for his writing, it was also an opportunity to change this pattern for his life and for the good of his soul.

Structure in memoir is not something that can be easily imposed from outside; it has to come from within the story of your life as you see it. The structure you uncover might be the one that you need and it might be very different from what you originally imagined. These 'turning points' can help you to see that and so choose the structure that feels most vital to your writing. No one can tell you what structure to use. You have to discover it for yourself.

And this brings us to another point. Memoir is never just about you. Autobiography can be all about you and, if you are famous, it will be fascinating, or illuminating, or even both. Memoir is always about you as the observer of a situation. The story of 'how I dodged the draft of the Vietnam War' is, if it's well written, the story of what you observed as you lived through those times, how those times affected everyone and what it must have felt like for the many people who took this route to avoid having to kill or be killed. The fact that you have lived through something unusual or difficult is not enough to make a real memoir. You may have survived the most horrific adventures, yet if you can't make the readers care about your plight, if you can't let them see that you are some sort of representative for at least some of those who cannot speak, then the memoir becomes a somewhat self-indulgent diary. Primo Levi's *Survival in Auschwitz* is a shocking eyewitness account of what happened to the minds and souls of those who were incarcerated with him. He observes, he questions, he wonders, he notes what he has to do himself in order to survive, yet he does so not as a person who demands pity but as a writer who wishes to make sense of what happened by recording it without sentimentality. He says comparatively little about himself, his family, his loves and his hopes. His companions are killed or die of disease and he notices the strange happenstances that meant that the strongest often died when the weak managed to scrape by. So, as you write, please consider this carefully: this memoir is certainly your story, seen through your eyes. Yet it is never going to be only about you. You are there as the eyes and ears for someone else, for the readers who will want to know what it is you went through so that they can see their own struggles more clearly after having seen yours. You may say in reply to this that you'll never show your writing to anyone else, so this does not apply. I'll simply re-iterate my earlier point: you are there as the observer of yourself as you were at the time, and that is why it is useful to think about 'the reader', because you will be assessing your experience, not just re-creating it.

The second part of this exercise may prove beneficial, also. Take a moment and try to identify the major turning point in the lives of those people you found it difficult to deal with. See if you can find twelve points, otherwise do the best you can. Cull the twelve down to six and then to four. Ask the same questions you asked of your own experience. You may be surprised at what emerges.

Very often, when we look at other people's experiences through their eyes and not ours, their lives can have a coherence we might have missed otherwise. This can be particularly true of parents. We tend to assume, because they live in the same time period as we do, to some extent, that they can be assessed by the present sets of understandings. But this may not be the case. Many times writers have written about how they couldn't understand their parents until they carefully thought their way back into their parent's lives using exercises like this. Sometimes this was achieved by physically seeing the places where their parents grew up, for example, or by looking at photographs. One woman, who had struggled with her father's inability to talk to her about his feelings, began to make the connection that since her father was a World War Two veteran he just didn't want to talk about what he'd seen, or about any feelings that weren't upbeat. She saw this as a failing. Further research showed her that almost none of that generation in that demographic group thought it was acceptable to talk about the devastation and heartbreak of the time. It just wasn't what they did, for the most part. She thought he was withholding and remote, which he was; but he was that way because that was how people were expected to deal with the pain at that time.

At this point you may also be asking yourself what is the good in dredging up memories that may be painful? Or perhaps you're wondering how you can insert the memories you've located into the memoir you had planned. You may even be asking whether you want to continue with your writing at all. So I'd like to put in a personal word that may help you, and it's one that arose as a direct result of a writer asking me why I chose to teach memoir, especially as there are already so many of them out there, already published, awaiting our attention. Why would I choose to encourage people to write more? Isn't that a little like taking coals to Newcastle, or sending ice to Greenland?

I've had some years to think about this and I feel the question has three answers, each of which is linked. The first reason we write memoir is because there is so much information that gets lost. We don't know what we don't know. A grandparent dies and we discover, much later, that we never knew the names of our great-grandparents, nor where they came from. I was reminded of this when I traveled to Switzerland to see my relatives and to introduce them to my then girlfriend. My uncle decided to take us on a walk through his hometown. As my girlfriend knew nothing about the Swiss part of my family my uncle painstakingly explained various details of family history: there was the town hall at which my grandfather had worked for fifty years; there was my grandfather's mother's house, and she was related to.... And so on. I walked along, astonished. No one had ever bothered to explain these things to me. It was assumed that I knew them – when not only did I *not* know but also I had long ago forgotten to ask about them. The grandparents I knew had always been old, slightly deaf, and hard to communicate with since they spoke a Swiss-German dialect and my German (*Ho'h Deutsch*, as they called it) was rudimentary, at best. So I'd never really spoken with them at all. I simply did not know very much about these people and now, long after they were dead, I very much wanted to. Without a certain amount of basic information it's very hard to feel that one knows one's history at all. For many writers, preserving that history is an important goal. As we've seen with the adolescents who had pictures of themselves taken next to buildings they had lived in, this sort of research can provide a sense of where one stands in the course of time and history. It can be both illuminating and humbling in the best possible way – our egos are reduced in the process to something less than their noisy clamorous selves.

The second reason we write memoir, and the one that has even more value for the writer, is because in re-visiting the stories that make up our lives we place ourselves on the path of healing. So many writers I have worked with have been moved to write memoir because they wanted to ask direct questions about their lives, questions that had to do with hurt. These questions needed to be addressed so the individuals could feel whole again. One woman wrote specifically to explore questions about what had happened to her memories between the ages of six and twelve. Why could she not remember that time? All she knew was that she had been taken into a foster home and then later adopted, in the process unfortunately being separated from her siblings. She knew, viscerally, that this period of time had been blanked out of her memory because she had probably been frightened and angry. This was the part of her that needed to be reclaimed, healed, and resolved so that she could be fully herself. As she wrote she began noticing that she had been trying very hard at that time to be 'good' so that someone would come along and rescue her. She had, in fact, had to fight daily to repress her fear, her anger and her anxiety so that she could be pleasant and acceptable to those adults she was terrified would abandon her if she showed any of her true feelings. I could add many more stories to this one and they'd all say the same thing – that writing our life stories can bring us to a place where we recover enough of our histories so that we can achieve psychic healing; and every moment of pain experienced along the way is felt only in order to be able to let it go.

The third reason for going through this lengthy process of writing is that it can take both reader and writer to a place of real wisdom. We have to be able to see our lives fully before we can truly start to understand what it means to be alive and to have lived our lives. And when we reach understanding we let go of judgments and condemnations and anger. Ultimately all memoir writing is about love. We cannot write a bitter, vengeful memoir and also have it be true and wise; it may be entertaining, but it won't be wise. What we discover, again and again, is that writers will face some harrowing aspect of their lives and yet not want to condemn or punish the people who caused the pain. They are much more likely to feel compassion. Writers who have faced issues as painful as sexual and physical abuse are much more likely to ask how they can prevent it happening to others than to think up new ways to punish the offenders. They can do this because they have felt the pain and moved through the experience to a place of real wisdom. That wisdom comes from a place of love, a place of optimism that the world we know can be made better, can be healed, and that 'my' story is only important if it can contribute to that healing by making others aware of what needs to be done. And so, if you let it, your memoir will lead you, inevitably, to a place of love. Memoir writing starts with you and then it leads to a place of love; and everyone can identify with the healing power of love. This is how the soul work gets done.

It will come as no real surprise to you, then, that memoir writing has these three levels, just as great art does. The first is always anchored in the personal, in detailed observation, in those moments when we say, as readers 'Yes, I can see that scene.' This is one reason we have the Treasure Chest – so that the physical details are saved. If the narrative you produce does not feel real, if the words you write do not seem to be anchored in observed fact, the reader will stop paying attention and to some extent, you as writer, will have slipped away from the actual to the imagined or the evasive. Why? Because the effect will be of vagueness, and vagueness never feels vital to anyone. We're likely to read something that is imprecise and find ourselves asking questions, annoyed that the writer has not spelled out specifics, doubting whether or not the writer knows what she is writing. Soul work demands precision, or the Unconscious begins to feel that we are just going through the motions. This first level of writing is vitally important, and it depends upon well-chosen words, careful observation, and scrupulous honesty.

When we have that first level of writing under control we'll see that our story, whatever it is, is always linked to some aspect of a larger social story. The story of an abused child is in one sense the story of every abused child, and it matters in order that we can be aware of it and help to prevent it in future; it also alerts us to the huge psychic cost to that person and to all who are touched by her.

And when we are alert to this broader sense of the story as history we have a chance, just a chance, that the memoir will be able to illuminate for the writer and for the reader some of the deep values of the psyche, those aspects of our selfhood we share with others and that lurk deeper than we care to look during our daily lives. We may find ourselves looking at the whole drama in which we have played – and perhaps continue to play – a part, and see that we have been cast into a role that we never before understood. What does this mean? An example could be the woman in a recent workshop who found great relief when she recognized that her family had cast her in the classic role of the scapegoat. She had been made to carry all the injury and sadness for decades *and had accepted it*. Once she saw how this worked, she was able to refuse to play the role any more and was able to free herself from the past. In doing so, she was also able to see why her family had felt the need to scapegoat at all. She described the recognition as 'releasing'. She no longer felt crazy, or 'bad', or inadequate, though the rest of the family, of course, didn't get it. But that didn't matter to her: she was writing her way to freedom.

Notes

1. Aristotle, *Poetics*. Widely reprinted.
2. Sophocles, *Oedipus Rex* and *Antigone*. Widely reprinted.
3. Primo Levi, *Survival in Auschwitz: The Nazi Assault on Humanity*, Free Press 1961.

Chapter Ten

The Fall from Grace and the Fall into Grace: What can you learn from disaster?

In the previous chapter I gave the example of the woman who discovered that, all her life, she'd unconsciously been playing the role of the scapegoat for her family's dysfunction and how that recognition brought her to a new place. What I'm going to suggest here is that there are many different ways we can be damaged as we grow up, and that where we stumble is where we will become stronger – if we are able to recognize it. In ancient myths we frequently come across tales in which a character stumbles, or his plough is caught on a ring as he works the field and, when he pulls on the ring, he finds a cave full of riches waiting for him (Joseph Campbell refers to this symbol cycle within 'The Arabian Nights' legends). The mythic value of this plot detail is: it's only when we hit an obstacle that we are forced to descend into ourselves, and when we do that the riches of the deep psyche are waiting for us. They're down there, waiting for us to claim them and make our lives wonderful, but we can't get to them unless we suffer a challenge first. The challenge is always one that upsets the ordinary, comforting status quo, which then forces us to reassess where we are in our lives.

Now, usually we think in terms of the phrase 'falling *from* grace', that point in our lives when things went wrong and our luck changed. I'd like you to take a moment now and consider how, for many of us, that time of change might in fact be a real gift, which caused us to face our lives in a new way; and, of course, we learn more from disasters than from successes. Often the disasters in our lives have real gifts for us; we can, and do, fall *into* grace at such times.

Several people I've worked with have pointed to major reverses in their lives, points when they felt they'd thrown away all their chances, or perhaps times when serious illnesses caused them to have to reshape their lives drastically. In each instance they have said that these were times that led to the sorts of reassessments that allowed them to remake their lives. The woman who became ill with a disease that the doctors, one after another, declared was incurable, was indeed at her lowest point. Without medical insurance, without the ability to hold down a job, and without any hope of a way forward she was wondering whether life was worth living at all. Then, quite suddenly, something shifted for her. She decided that the doctors' diagnoses were simply unacceptable and there had to be another way forward. She just didn't want to keep living in pain. So she started to explore yoga, meditation, T'ai Chi and other healing modalities. She mobilized her enormous willpower and devoured books on healing, went to classes, went to a stream of alternative doctors, talked to everyone she could find who had some sort of knowledge she felt she could use. Three years later – three difficult and agonizing years later – she was free of her illness. She was also a completely new person in terms of her outlook on life. She'd seen that life was not about staying with the job she had, which paid well but which she hated, and that there might be other things within her that needed more self-expression than her paid work allowed. She began to write every day, and she rediscovered herself as a visual artist, too, which was something she'd put on hold for years. She was expressing the pain that had led, indirectly, to her illness and her collapse and, as she did so, she was letting go of that old way of being.

The changes had not only been hers, however; her children had seen her suffering and been deeply frightened, yet they had not given up or run away. Instead they learned about courage and determination from her, and they learned about how important it is to refuse to be in victim-mode, a mode where one remains simply accepting the dire prognoses of the largely patriarchal medical establishment. Her husband, also, was changed by this time period and he discovered that simply being present and continuing to be loyal had a power all its own – he hadn't realized he could be so loyal. He also hadn't known he could love so deeply. This is what she saw, and it was indeed 'a blessing in disguise'.

I could add many more instances to this specific example, and all would show the same thing. Sometimes it is the disasters that happen in our lives that show us the real qualities we have. Frequently they lead us to profound insight and wisdom. For the woman in this example life was immeasurably enhanced by what might have destroyed her. She described the situation as learning the hard way – because she simply wouldn't have been able to learn unless the lessons had been hard ones, she said. I was delighted when I heard her say that, because it seems to me that often we only change when we are forced to, when the world roughs us up enough so that we take notice. This is how most people are. We won't see the way ahead. We refuse to change what we do even though we know it's a bad idea. We cling on to the old sense of self even when it's no longer working. This is the essential human dilemma, and it's well worth writing about.

Writing about such events can be painful, of course. Not writing about them, not thinking about them, may be a way of not acknowledging the pain; but it means we can never learn from it either.

As you think about your memoir now, is there a Fall from Grace that actually led you to more understanding? I would be surprised if there isn't. And that would be, quite possibly, at the center of your memoir. It might not be something you want to write about, perhaps because you're not proud of the events or the attitudes. Yet memoir writing is not about pride, and it's not about making yourself look good. It's about finding out what's true.

Notes

1. Joseph Campbell. The Arabian Nights Legends are mentioned in the PBS series tape 2, op. cit.

Chapter Eleven

What Can I Say in my Memoir?
What if Someone gets Upset? The Six Stages each
Memoir, and each Memoir writer, will go through

By now I hope you are fairly well along in terms of putting words onto a page on a regular basis – preferably every day. As you do so you'll find yourself asking all sorts of questions about the whole process, such as: Can I really say that? What if my mother reads this? Is this material that I need to include in the memoir? Am I allowed to say these things about these people? Will they sue me? What if I've remembered it wrongly?

Many writers lose a great deal of sleep worrying about these items, so it's not a bad idea to address them before they get out of hand and before they undermine the writing process. Let's take the one that seems to surface most often – a general fear that someone somewhere will be offended and seek retribution for perceived slanders. The first thing to do with a fear like this is to welcome it and turn it around. If you were going to write the sort of memoir that would leave everyone smelling like roses, then I'd suggest you'd have no story worth reading. Life is about many things, but one of the most compelling of these is conflict. So if you find yourself thinking this way it's a pretty good sign that you know you have something worth saying that actually needs to be said. Your take on events has, obviously, not been accepted or believed by those most closely involved, and now you're putting the record straight. This sense of fear – that you'll offend someone – is actually a statement about your courage. You know that you want to be truthful and that, perhaps, this will not sit well with others. So value your courage, first of all.

In addition the question raises an important thought: that it considers others as able to shut you down. Do not be deceived. Others cannot shut you down or shut you up. Only you can do that. So don't give your pre-conscious the chance to censor you before you've got started.

If you find yourself with the book contract ready to sign, the pen poised, and your agent whispering about six figure advances, that will be the time to think about whether or not you've been as fully kind to the people you describe as you'd like to be. That will be the time when your publisher's lawyers will consult with you and the fact checkers will ask respectful questions because they don't want another James Frey incident on their hands. You may recall that Frey's memoir *A Million Little Pieces* was at first praised by Oprah and then, when she discovered that large amounts of it were not historically accurate, she demanded a public apology. Unless you have fabricated major parts of your memoir, you need not be concerned. If you have invented sections you can still call it a novel, of course. But this is all a long way off as yet and it is the only time you'll need to worry about what other people think, so for right now get on and do the writing. And above all, don't fall into this temptation of worrying about others people's views, because it is merely another way to censor yourself. Later, when you re-read, you may decide that you've been a shade harsh with some characters whose names you may choose to change as a result. My experience has been that any writer who really cares about writing finds that the memoir is not about getting even or kiss-and-tell. It's much more likely that writing out your life will bring you to a place of greater understanding about those who have hurt you and you may, in fact, wind up blessing your enemies for the obstacles they provided that you were able to overcome. A good model for this is Barack Obama's memoir *Dreams from My Father*. Obama was actually a lawyer at the time he wrote this memoir and so he'd have been aware of any legal issues. In his introductory comments he says that he has changed some names in order to protect the privacy of some of the people who appear in his book, and in some instances he has rolled events together, but he has attempted to be accurate as far as memory allows. Here are his actual words:

> Finally, there are the dangers inherent in any autobiographical work: the temptation to color events in ways favorable to the writer, the tendency to overestimate the interest one's experiences hold for others, selective lapses of memory. Such hazards are only magnified when the writer lacks the wisdom of age; the distance that can cure one of certain vanities. I can't say that I've avoided all, or any, of these hazards successfully. Although much of this book is based on contemporaneous journals or the oral histories of my family, the dialogue is necessarily an approximation of what was actually said or relayed to me. For the sake of compression, some of the characters that appear are composites of people I've known, and some events appear out of precise chronology. With the exception of my family and a handful of public figures, the names of most characters have been changed for the sake of privacy.
>
> Whatever the label that attaches to this book – autobiography, memoir, family history, or something else – what I've tried to do is write an honest account of a particular province of my life.

How elegantly he puts it! He doesn't avoid the problems inherent in memoir, he simply says, look, this is what I did and why. We can gain strength from this straightforward approach. A woman in one of my workshops agonized over whether she could accurately recall conversations that had occurred three decades earlier, and was she allowed to invent the words? The answer to this is simple. Always be as accurate as you can be, and if you cannot be, and if there is no objective evidence, then you are quite entitled to say something like, 'the way I remember that day is....' Memoir is to some extent always going to be about the shifting sands of memory, and it is actually praiseworthy to acknowledge that the words we use are fugitive, and that anyhow, memoir is in this respect a bit like standing in a shower of rain trying to juggle odd-shaped objects that are made of dissolving soap. No one can ever get it perfectly right under those circumstances, yet we can give a true impression, make a powerful gesture, at what the events were and how they affected us.

Frederick Buechner, in his three part memoir *The Sacred Journey*, *Now and Then*, and *Telling Secrets* quite frequently stops the flow of narrative to ask whether he is doing the correct thing. Here he is in *Now and Then*:

> How much do you put into an account like this? What do you put in? How differently your life sounds, feels, tastes, when you are living it from the way it sounds when you write it down with all the day-to-dayness of it forgotten and left out. On paper it sounds as if you knew where you were going and why you were going there and kept at it.

It's not the only time he does this, and yet the effect on the reader is one of intimacy, as if he has looked us in the eye to say: what actually is a memoir, and how can I be sure I'm doing it right? This feels much more honest than those writers who expect us to take only one side of an issue and see everything their way. That is when I feel as if I'm having my arm twisted to accept their self-justifications. Again, if you're worried about accuracy, turn that worry into something more constructive. It's telling you that you are engaged in a serious task, one that involves being as fair to everyone and every event as you can manage, and that you want to get it right. Good. That is a most worthy aim and you must not let it silence you in any way. Accept the fear as a reminder that you are undertaking a task that has to be as true as possible. Yours is an important story, otherwise you'd have no worries about it. Your conscience and your soul require you to be as truthful as possible.

Sometimes writers find that this desire to tell the truth spills over into the rest of their lives. They start saying what they mean more often. They start to live a little more boldly, more authentically. They use words to get somewhere rather than to avoid getting somewhere. If you find yourself doing this it may feel uncomfortable at first. You may find yourself saying things like, 'They'll just have to deal with me saying what I think today,' or you will find yourself saying no to things that previously you'd have just grinned and done anyway, while finding yourself feeling imposed upon. You'll find you'll ask for what you need, you'll call in favors that no one ever thought would be called in, and you'll make space for yourself. Relish this change. This is part of the soul work you are doing. After all, we are not here to make people happy by deferring to them all. We are here to be authentically ourselves. Joseph Campbell put this beautifully when he said, "Jesus said we were to love our enemies. He didn't say we weren't to have enemies." We are not here to be walked upon. We can love our enemies, understand them, respect them as human beings; and we must know that in all probability they'll still be our enemies.

As we observed right at the start of this book, writing your memoir will change you; and your fears about telling your truths are indicative that the change is happening. It's difficult to spell out how much you will change – that will depend on how hard you work – but one of the reasons I have taught memoir and personal writing for so many years is because I know that writing one's life does cause change, and I love it for that reason. I've already described how, when I was teaching in the Massachusetts prisons, I worked with Kenny Wightman on his life story. As things turned out the movie was never made and the memoir has still not been published, even though huge amounts of money had been poured into the movie part of the operation. But what I saw after we moved beyond the excitement was a man who was re-assessing his life. He told me things that he wasn't proud of; and he told me things that he found himself wondering about. Why had he done the things he'd done, he asked, over and over again, reflecting that it seemed like another life, someone else's, not his. In the process he changed. He was changing anyway – he'd decided to take a productive way forward in his life behind bars. Yet what he was able to do by looking at his past in this way was to accelerate the process, deepen it, and move to a better space. He's out now and determined to live a law-abiding life. He's doing well, and he knows that, to some extent, writing his life story was part of that.

Since you too will change, I will spell out to you what you can expect as you travel this road. Personal growth moves through six distinct stages. These are life stages, but they are also stages that we go through whenever we start a new task. Writers have noted them implicitly for thousands of years and they are the subject of my book *Stories We Need to Know*. You can read the book if you want a more detailed assessment of what the stages are, and where they came from. For now, though, we'll consider the stages as they reflect your progress. The six stages are: The Innocent; The Orphan; The Pilgrim; The Warrior-Lover; The Monarch; and The Magician.

Let's look at these more closely.

The Innocent is the stage at which you are just beginning to think about memoir. You haven't written a memoir before. Perhaps you haven't written anything much before, and have read only a few other writers in this genre. And so to begin with you are likely to appear at a class or workshop, or pick up this book, thinking, OK, these people will show me how to do this if I just pay attention. Approaching the task with trust you'll be convinced the world is run by understandable rules, that what you have to say will be welcomed, and that advice will be forthcoming. At this life stage writers frequently come to me and ask, "How should I do this?" as if there were only one way, and as if I knew their life sufficiently well to be able to make a half-way decent pronouncement that could guide them. Some even hand me a sheaf of untidy papers, asking if I can put some sort of order into them. And this may be on the very first meeting! It's almost impossible to make satisfactory editing decisions under those circumstances. As I tell people, I don't know what they don't know about themselves yet, so how can I proceed? I have to be very gentle, because people at the Innocent stage are extending considerable trust, and are vulnerable, and it takes courage to make this first step. The Innocent is wonderful to deal with, as she will tend to put me on a pedestal, which is always nice, and will listen to all I say. And so I have to be very careful about the advice I give, since I know that my job is not to be on any sort of pedestal, but to work with the writer as she discovers her own voice and her own strengths. For even the most experienced writer will find a new voice for each project, just as a singer finds a new and appropriate key for each song.

The Innocent may, for example, assume that a memoir has to begin at birth and proceed in an orderly fashion until the present moment. While this is logical it misses the most important aspect of memoir, which is that it can be a selection of events, and may even be a selection that focuses on a few key months – or days - rather than a whole life span. There are countless memoirs that do not start at the beginning, and some of them even start at the end, asking how the author got to this place. Many of them jump to and fro in time, and are the richer for it. Vladimir Nabokov's memoir *Speak Memory* is almost the complete reverse of what anyone would have expected of a celebrity memoir, and it barely mentions his writing at all! Yet it is an intriguing examination of the way memory works. To the Innocent, especially, it is a shock.

The writer graduates from being an Innocent when she discovers that neither I nor any teacher has all the answers, although I may have a way of getting her to find her own answers – which is much more valuable. This writer is most likely now to move into the second stage, which is The Orphan.

The Orphan knows that the world isn't going to provide any easy answers and that this project may require more effort and emotional heavy lifting than the Innocent had expected. The Orphan, just like all of us who find ourselves without parental support, will look for a safe place to be 'adopted' while the writing goes ahead. This is the writer who may very well play safe, writing only things which are light and non-threatening in an effort to keep on everyone's good side. Sometimes those with a flare for comedy will do exceptionally well at this, and yet, the Orphan is trying to fit in, and is very likely to ask herself what models she can copy, what tricks can she use, what stance can she take, what the 'correct' way to do something might be – which is very different from the writer who lets the process tell her how the story needs to be written. There is, of course, nothing wrong with being an Orphan writer. Many people have been very successful in delivering memoirs that are exactly what they know the public will lap up. Yet just as the Orphan can't afford to risk offending anyone in the adoptive environment, sometimes one finds memoirs that don't, actually, have anything to say aside from the events they describe. There is no sense of the writer having come to a place of wisdom. We leave such memoirs feeling short-changed, although we may have been entertained along the way. Memoirs written (sometimes ghost written) by athletes occasionally have that effect on me. The Orphan writer is usually the one who asks how to do things, what trends to imitate, and is one who wants to know what things will sell. These are important considerations, but only in so far as they are to be in service to the main task of telling the truth as one feels it.

Sooner or later the Orphan breaks free and decides to take some risks. At this point she is ready to experiment, to go where the writing takes her, to explore. She will say things like, "I wanted to write about my mother, but I found myself having to write about the picnic with my cousin instead...." When a writer becomes aware that not all the processes she is involved with are fully conscious, she releases the tight control that dominates the Orphan's world and she becomes, instead, a Pilgrim. This is the third stage.

The Pilgrim as we all know is a person who goes off on a journey or a quest knowing the general goal, but not sure what she will meet along the way, let alone how she'll feel about the goal when she gets there. This is the writer who is prepared to listen to her life, and let it reveal its form to her. She will have a sense of what the main thrust of the story is. Just like a true Pilgrim, she'll have a direction, a sense of what the major themes and events are going to be, and yet she'll be ready to stay open to what comes along during the process. The Pilgrim may find herself writing sections that don't seem to link up, and will ask me, How do I link this? What's the reason I keep going off on these tangents? The answer, of course, is that these aren't tangents at all. They are just the demands the story makes, and the overall pattern will emerge later, perhaps much later. As the Pilgrim begins to sense more strongly the true focus of her tale she will eventually declare what she is going to concentrate on, and so becomes what I term a Warrior-Lover.

The Warrior-Lover is aptly named. Just as a Warrior can't fight unless she believes in the cause and loves it enough to fight for it, so a lover who is not prepared to fight for her love is not worth much. The two aspects, love and determination, are key to any memoir writer. This is the point at which the writer feels a strong desire to tell her story, to take the risks of telling it true, but not because she wants to beat someone up in print, but because the love of truth is stronger than anything else. It's important to note the sense of balance this will require. The temptation is for the writer to become all Warrior and force her views down everyone's throats. 'I'm going to tell it like it is!' may sound like a fine and praiseworthy sentiment, but it can lead to overly forceful writing, the sort of writing that leaves the reader no room to make up his or her own mind. The old dictum of fiction writing is, 'Show, don't tell.' It's an approach that allows the reader to see, and then reach his or her own conclusions. In memoir the same rule is worth remembering, 'Reveal, don't make declarations.' I've worked with writers who would say things like, "I really told it in this section" and my response in these situations tends to be rather simple. I'll ask whether the reader has been told in such a way so as to be able to hear, or whether the writer was doing the telling for her own sense of satisfaction. I think most of us are happier when meanings are revealed, not stated. And there is never just one side to reality: there are doubts and there are questions about almost anything. The second temptation at this archetypal level is to be too much the Lover side of the balanced duo. This is the writer who always presents the Pollyanna version of everything. While this can make for engaging and uplifting episodes in any book – and one of my favorites of this type is Gerald Durrell's *My Family And Other Animals* – one leaves these memoirs feeling as if one has been treated to an evening with a marvelous raconteur, but without getting to the soul behind the social pose, nor coming fully to grips with the experience of being alive at that time. Life is all a joke when viewed from this point of view. Compare this to the words of one of my students who said, quite humbly, "I don't know. I can only chronicle."

Writers at Warrior-Lover level display tremendous energy and courage in doing what they need to do with their life stories. One woman who needed to discover details about her mother's life, and who was getting stone-walled by relatives, decided that she couldn't allow that to get in her way and so she put an advertisement in the local paper of the town her mother had died in, asking for information. The ad generated a few responses, all of them useful, and a photograph of her mother's fifth grade class, which she felt was a real treasure. It also caught the attention of the paper's freelance reporter who decided he wanted to write a piece about her search for her mother, and in turn that generated some more responses. The woman was delighted and said it was as if, until that point, she didn't really and completely feel her mother had existed at all, but now she had old ladies and gentlemen telling her that, yes, they'd known her mother well enough to say hello, and so on. In real terms it was little enough, but in psychological terms it was a huge boost. The Warrior-Lover in her was not going to be put off or made to give up. She went forward, boldly. The writing she produced became superb, since it was charged with this same energy.

Just as any Warrior has to pick the important battles and refuse to fight others, so the Warrior-Lover has to select with care which episodes to write about, which to lavish love and care upon, and which need to be released. This means being aware of how much is enough to get a point across, and also to achieve a balance. It is at this stage that the writer begins to appreciate the need for delicacy, tact, and careful wording in a new way. Forceful writing has its place, and persuasive writing does, also.

When the writer begins to understand this about her own writing and her own life (and it can be considerably easier to achieve this balance when writing about another person's life rather than one's own) she is ready to graduate to the next level, which I call the Monarch.

The Monarch is an even mix of the twin attributes of the King and Queen, as seen in stereotypical terms. The King is traditionally all executive decision and force; the Queen is more compassionate and nurturing. Ideally both sets of attributes coalesce in one person. When this happens the writer reaches a new level of mastery that depends less upon including every detail (which is what the eager Orphan will tend to do) and more upon being able to select the important events and the relevant details so the reader can complete the picture. T.S. Eliot called this the ability to find the 'objective correlative' in poetry. By this he meant the significant details of life that can, by being selected, rise to a greater suggestiveness and importance. One doesn't need to explain the value of such details to a reader since, if they have been chosen with care, they will carry their message on their own. Another way of putting it might be to say that at this point the writer is ready to think in terms of repeated motifs, symbols, and recurrent imagery that somehow seem to run through one's life. In *Bird by Bird* Anne Lamott describes how when reviewing a first draft she will look out specifically for these recurring images, noting how they may be conveying something of importance that she was not consciously aware of as she wrote the first rough draft. In these images, she says, can be found the heart of what is really asking to be communicated. Like watching for one's own subliminal messages where, embedded in those words that were chosen for a slightly different purpose, there are riches to be found. All of us, if we choose to analyze our language usage objectively, can be surprised by the unexpected prejudices and biases it reveals. The Monarch is aware of this and explores it to see what is really happening below the surface.

What this meant for one of my writers was that a chance description suddenly became central to her memoir. In one of the opening passages of her memoir she described how as a young girl she was struggling through a snowstorm down a path that was a shortcut through a cemetery. She was unable to reach her objective, the hospital where her mother was, and the snow was falling so fast that she could not see the way ahead at all. She was in real danger of freezing to death, but found her way back to safety by walking, "in my own footsteps". That phrase became the title of her memoir and in it she saw something that described the scope of her life. She saw that she had wanted from her earliest years to connect with her mother, and that everything had conspired against that wish until she was forced to save her own life, and her sanity, by paying attention to her own inner sense of direction. That inner knowledge would take her back to who she was, away from a self-destructive longing for her mother. We see this symbolized in the phrase, 'in my own footsteps' as she guides herself back to safety. The resonance is also, of course, with the sense that writing a memoir means to some extent going over the ground one has traveled so that the journey can be understood more fully. As I've described it here it may seem difficult to follow. You'd have to read the whole memoir to see the real quality of this significant detail which she was able to identify, and so appreciate the way a very few words can convey the depth and scope of the experience.

It is for this reason that the Monarch can rarely be seen in the early stages of writing. It is an archetype that emerges in the writer usually when revising the text and asking the massively important question - so what have I got here? Just as a ruler in a Kingdom has to decide whom to trust, so does the writer have to decide what material is trustworthy. In order to be at this stage a writer has to have achieved a fairly high level of competence and assurance. By the time you've written an entire first draft you should be about ready to bring this part of yourself forward. It is, in some ways, the metacognitive aspect of any writer, the part that thinks about the way one uses one's thinking and considers the attitudes the writer has of herself. An example may be useful, here. In one of my books I found, only on reading the page proofs, that I frequently referred to love at certain points as being 'ferocious'. At first I thought I had been lazy and repetitive. After a while I recognized that my word choice was trying to convey something to me that I hadn't really been alert to before – that the type of love I was describing was primal, almost frightening in its power. I hadn't been able to say that, directly. Now, reviewing the page proofs, I knew I had to acknowledge that I was writing about more than I had been prepared to admit.

In psychological terms we can see this as the emerging sense of an observer ego. Used carefully this figure will ask important questions about the value of the work you have done in terms of inquiring about what needs to be conveyed to an audience. This includes questions like, what do the readers really need to know here? I sometimes feel that if more writers reached this level of self-awareness we'd have fewer narratives of the look-how-horrible-my-life-has-been variety, since the result of such writing is so very often to make the reader feel that the world is a horrible place full of meanness and ugliness that only a few souls can struggle through. The let-me-tell-you-how-bad-it-is writer is as dull as the person who always caps your conversational anecdote with one that's worse. "You think you had it bad? Well, listen to what I went through…" This is misery one-upmanship. And it is worthless. It is the action of the Orphan who is in love with his own misery, which he wears like a badge of rank, while the Monarch stands back and asks the larger questions about what it may all mean. Beware of writing that invites us as readers into a place of misery – that tends to be what the Orphan will produce and I'm not sure that writing in order to depress one's audience is a particularly useful aim anyway. Writing to empower one's audience is far better – and that is what the Monarch does.

In the larger world the Monarch never speaks in the voice of the ego. The Queen of England does not use 'I' in public utterance. She uses 'we' because she represents, symbolically at least, not just a person but also the whole country itself. Writers can do well if they remember this. Ideally you are not writing just for you, but for the good of everyone concerned. You may have to speak unpleasant truths but this will be in the service of revealing wisdom, *your* wisdom that is worth sharing.

When this happens the writer can become, if only for a moment, a **Magician**. This is the final stage. Just as Magicians and Wizards of days gone by used magic spells (*spell* is derived from the Anglo-Saxon for 'word' as in God's spell, which later became Gospel) so you will be capable of using words to convey something far more important than just information. You'll be conveying insight. And that is when words can move us to tears or to joy – an astonishing, everyday example of magic.

The Magician needs to use the right spell, and the correct words, treated with care. And so does the writer. It's about more than persuasion, more than argumentation; it's about being able to make the words convey something that can only be conveyed that way. Milan Kundera put it beautifully when he said that it is the duty of the novel to convey in words what can only be conveyed in words.

The implication is that if its values can be conveyed in any other way then it probably isn't pushing forward the limits of our understanding. Your Memoir, when it reaches this stage, will resonate within the heart of your readers in a way that will be very hard to analyze clinically or boil down to a fifty word blurb for the back of the book's cover. If it can be reduced to fifty words then it should be, and we can all save time. But if it's worth reading it's worth reading every word. One of my favorite lines about this is from a Woody Allen film, in which a character played by Allen announces that he's taken a speed-reading course. It works really well he says, glowing with self-importance; "I read *War and Peace* in twenty minutes. It involves Russia." It's not what is said that matters, on many occasions; it's what has been suggested and conveyed less directly that moves us so we remember. It's the experience you've provided for the reader that will be important. The secrets of the human heart can't be spelled out by mathematical formulae, but they can be suggested, and evoked, by a scene that is presented before us with care.

The Magician is present in the person who reports that the writing took over, and that she found herself writing about things she never expected to. This is what happens when the individual sits at the desk or keyboard and the words just seem to pour out, and they're all important words, too. This is when the Unconscious has taken charge, but in a controlled way. Remember, the Monarch's job is to manage the kingdom so all the citizens can be fully themselves, doing whatever they do, producing whatever it is they produce, and if the Monarch succeeds in that, she becomes this Magician figure. When you trust yourself, your Unconscious, and your writing, and you let them do what they need to do, then the Magic happens.

Your memoir will take you through these six stages as you write it – if you let it be written the way it needs to be written – and it will lead you and your readers to a place of understanding, of compassion, of wisdom. And if it does so it will have contributed enormously to the amount of peace on this planet. That is not a trivial goal. It will also bring you to a place of peace.

These six stages are not just an invention. They are actual definable stages that I have watched writers go through on their way to mastery of a writing project. Almost everyone manages to do so, even if they do not become Magicians in other aspects of their lives. I have taken this opportunity to write about them now because it can be immensely comforting to any writer to know that he or she is not just on a treadmill for producing a certain number of pages in a specific format. You are on a road and there are certain mileposts you will see as you go down it; and knowing what they are and how many there are can remind you about the nature of your task. Any decent how-to manual works the same way. Whether it has to do with home repairs or how to meditate, all will tell you what you can expect to find at different points. This is, essentially, no different. For our purposes, though, writing your life story can lead you to a place of peace and understanding, and I cannot imagine a more worthwhile task in life. This is the Soul Work we all have to do if we are to be fully authentic human beings.

These six archetypes can be useful in another way as well. They are a way for you to monitor your progress as you go through your writing, certainly, and they can also be a structure that you can use in creating a shape for your memoir. Whenever we start anything new we are, for a moment, Innocents, and then we move through all the stages. Starting off in your memoir you will be, to some extent, describing yourself as an Innocent who has run up against a few problems. 'The day my mother died was three days after my 13ᵗʰ birthday…' This is the start of a life story in which the world of someone, who is relatively unsuspecting, is turned upside down with results she could not have predicted; the Innocent is abruptly thrown into the cruel world as an Orphan (perhaps literally in this case!) This writer could choose to shape the narrative by showing the many confusions of the Orphan, following this with the search for the parental figures the Orphan craves, and then describing the yearning for the more meaningful connection that energizes the Pilgrim. This would then lead to the attainment of such connections in the Warrior-Lover, who then, in turn, is able to become wise enough to advise and help others as a Monarch. Perhaps the memoir itself is the way this person will help others.

The Six Archetypes probably work so well because they describe the deep structures of the human psyche, and as such they can be as useful to us as the concepts of childhood, adolescence, maturity and old age, except in this instance they correspond to inner development and not just the aggregation of years.

If you wish, you can take the episodes of your life that you know you want to include in the memoir and sort them out into these six archetypal categories. What you'll find is that we frequently slip back to earlier stages of development. We fall in love and, each time we do, we slip temporarily into the Innocent phase. How long we stay there is up to us. We move to a new country or a new state, and the same thing happens. Perhaps that causes us to make decisions we might otherwise have not made and this could be the structure of your memoir. However we wish to see them, these are six aspects of ourselves that we will want to know and understand better if we are to be fully present in this world, and that is part of our soul work, too.

Notes

1. James Frey's memoir became a sensation when Oprah made it her book club selection, and then when she learned that it was not entirely accurate she brought Frey onto her program again in order to tell him exactly how she felt about this.

2. Barack Obama, *Dreams from My Father; A Story of Race and Inheritance*, Three Rivers Press, 2004. p.xvi –xvii.

3. Frederick Buechner produced three books he calls memoirs, *The Sacred Journey; A Memoir of Early Days*, HarperOne 1991; *Now and Then; A Memoir of Vocation*, HarperOne 1991; and *Telling Secrets*, HarperOne 1992. The quoted extract is from *Now and Then*, p.32.

4. Joseph Campbell talks about loving one's enemies on many occasions. See the New Dimensions interviews with Michael Toms, *The Wisdom of Joseph Campbell*, Hay House, 1997,(4 CD set) for a full discussion.

5. *Stories We Need to Know; Reading Your Life Path in Literature* (Findhorn Press 2008) describes the six archetypes that have echoed through 3500 years of the western canon's finest literature.

6. Vladimir Nabokov, *Speak Memory; An Autobiography Revisited*, Vintage 1989.

7. Gerald Durrell, *My Family and Other Animals*, Penguin 1968

8. T.S. Eliot and 'the objective correlative'. The discussion first appears in 'Hamlet and his Problems' in *The Sacred Wood; Essays in Poetry and Criticism*, 1920.

9. Anne Lamott, *Bird By Bird; Some Instructions on Writing and Life*, Anchor 1995.

10. Milan Kundera, *The Art of the Novel*, Grove Press, 1988

11. Woody Allen. The quotation has been widely recorded, but originates in *Radio Days*, 1988.

Chapter Twelve

**Up Close and Personal:
What's Your Relationship to Your Memoir?**

At this point you'll have many ideas about what your memoir involves since you'll have memories emerging that you'll feel the need, perhaps the urgent desire, to write and explore. Good. But before you write some more, let's do another exercise.

This is a visualization exercise, and so you may want to read the words first and do the visualizing later. You can also have someone else read the exercise to you, as I suggested with the three gifts exercise in Chapter Six, or you can record it on tape and play it back when you have some quiet time.

So, first of all you will need to relax by sitting comfortably and, as before, focus on your breathing, feeling the smooth movement of your breath, in and out, and let all your other thoughts go. Sometimes I find it useful to count slowly as I do so. Breathe in, two, three, four, hold; breathe out, two, three, four, pause; breathe in, two, three, four. And so on. Counting, for me, stops my mind wandering and keeps me rooted in my breathing.

When you feel relaxed, imagine that you are getting ready to go to an entertainment of some sort. What are you wearing? Are you going to dress up? Spend a moment thinking about this. Visualize what you'll wear. Where will you be going? Do you know? Is it a surprise? A movie? A play? The opera? The circus?

It's now time to leave to get to the show. How do you travel? By bus? By limo? Do friends come and collect you? Do you walk? Is the night warm or cold? Be as specific as you want.

You arrive. What sort of place is it? What does it look like? Who is there? Do you walk upstairs? Do you enter an auditorium or something similar?

You look towards the stage or the place where the entertainment will be. What do you see? Does a curtain go up? If there are characters on stage, what are they doing? What are they saying? What is the action? Be as detailed as you can.

Take the time to write your responses and then to think about them. You may find this visualization has provoked a memory, in which case you may wish to write about that.

What I find when I do this exercise with groups is that the responses are as varied as one can imagine. Some people see themselves glamorously dressed going to the Oscar ceremony, where they're expecting an award. Others are going to see a rock band in an arena with 50,000 other fans. Many people see themselves going to a play, though, where the drama on the stage is, in some ways, a mirroring of their own personal drama. Sometimes people have reported watching scenes that, with very little analysis, correspond closely to the tensions they witnessed in their own homes growing up. So the point here is to ask yourself a few questions: What is the drama you are witnessing, and does it reflect your life? The second question is: what is your relationship to the action? Are you, for instance, way back in the auditorium, or up front, or unable to see clearly because there's something or someone in the way? Or perhaps you jump up on stage and get to be part of the action. The nature of the drama or show will be important; yet almost as important will be the distance between you and it. To some extent this distance will mirror the way you treat the material of your memoir. Are you somewhat remote from the action, an observer? Or are you up close? Or, as one man recorded, are you the person who gets up on the stage and rearranges the actors, setting them straight about a few things at the same time? I'm sure you can see that a life story written from the point of view of someone who is seeing things from a distance of time and years will be very different from the story of the person who still feels caught up in the swirl of the action. One perspective is not better than the other, but it is important for you as the writer to know roughly at what distance from events you feel most comfortable. This may be a clue to another important point - to what extent did you feel you were controlling the events in your life, and to what extent did they seem to be controlled by forces beyond your reach? You may need to write about that, too.

For most of us, when we look at events as being somehow distant from us, we are saying that in effect we were not directors of the action but we were acted upon, or we were observers. Those who, more rarely, feel themselves as a central part of the action, as the hero of their own drama, may think that everything is their doing. In truth it is probably neither of these cases, but it may be a version of them at different times. When I've done the exercise with groups, they have often been astounded at other people's visions of life. In fact most people assume that their own vision of life is the only sensible one, and everyone else's version is bizarre. In group work when readers have shared a piece of writing about an episode in which they were hurt, the response of other group members has been, on occasion, "Why didn't you just do so and so?" That question is logical yet it completely misses the point that sometimes we were so close to the action that we couldn't see other possibilities at that time. Later, after the heat of the moment has passed, we may be in a different relationship to the event, whatever it was.

One woman doing this visualization reported that she'd seen a play in which the family on stage had been involved in a vicious verbal fight, one that as a member of the audience she was helpless to prevent, even though she wanted to stand up and tell the actors to stop. Of course, she couldn't do that in a theater, she said, so she didn't. Not surprisingly she was able to link the visualization to her own family, and the way her mother and father would fight, which she felt herself to be completely powerless to do anything about even long after she was no longer a child in their home. It helped her to notice that she had always seen herself in this way, and that this was the lens through which she saw her entire life, not just her family experiences. This came as a jolt to her. It enabled her to ask necessary but uncomfortable questions. What would her life have been like if she'd felt she could interrupt those battling adults? How had that observer attitude affected her later life? There could be no easy answers to questions like these, yet I think these are exactly the kinds of questions we have to ask if we're going to make sure our personal soul work gets done. When there's a fight of any kind, even if we're just looking on, we are part of that central action. Perhaps the squabbling parents wouldn't have continued their fight if the woman had stood up and left? Perhaps part of the fight was that they needed her there to be an audience, so they could justify themselves in front of someone? These are uncomfortable questions, but they are necessary if we are to appreciate that, active or passive, we were a part of the actions that took place and that those actions have become part of who we are now.

A very different response to this visualization came from a young woman who related how she'd been to see a stage performance by the Blue Man Group – a mixture of dance, drumming, music, color, and fun that she thoroughly enjoyed, even the part where paint, which was part of the show and was poured over the tops of the steel drums, splashed everyone sitting in the first few rows. For her the choice of an actual event was not simply a case of her not paying attention to the instructions. She was able to write about how happy she was to be at an event with someone who really cared for her, and that this dynamic stage show could be innocent fun for everyone. It didn't include anything to make her feel depressed, she said, and still she felt it as emotionally moving. What this meant for her didn't emerge for a few days, but it was important, as she was expressing that in the past, when she'd felt excited or moved, it had tended to be by the negative emotions of fear, anger and depression. She'd go to hear rock bands expecting to come out feeling angry, ready to punch someone, as she thought that was just what people did. That was 'normal' for her; these were the emotions she thought were most real, while joy seemed to be an illusion. This visualization allowed her to recognize what she'd always known, that she actually could have fun, be moved and excited, and not feel destructive urges taking her over. Exploring this helped her to identify her attitudes from the past, and to accept that they didn't have to be that way. She was able to change her sense of what was possible for her life. Obviously this was a change that had already happened before she started writing. Yet, as we know, it's never enough to just change; it's also important to know *how* one has changed, and when, and what it means to us. Going to see Blue Man Group would therefore rank as one of the key moments of change in her life, and as such it would most likely be a key episode for her to include in her life writing.

Any time we are part of an event that we expect not to be much fun but which winds up by making us smile, we've altered the energy we brought with us and turned a negative into a positive. It signals a moment of change and is to be treasured.

This is in some ways a simple exercise yet I think you can see how it asks you to consider some vital questions about your relationship to events. Whatever you decide about that relationship is simply information that will help you see things in a new way. Remember, our biases are like our noses. We can see everyone else's but not our own. If you were simply writing an exciting narrative driven by external events, it wouldn't be vitally important to consider your idiosyncrasies as the recorder of events, because you'd be writing for the excitement and that would be the most important thing. If you are to do meaningful soul work you'll have, sooner or later, to look at your role in everything that happened around you. It's too easy to shrug our shoulders and say, look at all these crazy people! Aren't they weird? They're not like me, oh no....

The life lesson here is that to a great extent we cannot be fair to the people in our memoir until we have realized that we are a part of the problems we describe. As Deepak Chopra put it, 'You can't fix the world if you can't fix yourself.' It's always easy to point to the faults of others and to say that this is what caused things to fall apart, and yet that is almost always an evasion. We may not have been the main cause of the problem, but we were still part of it, I can guarantee you.

This exercise has been about starting you on the trajectory of thinking about your life in different ways, so let's continue to explore this for a moment. In Robertson Davies' wonderful novel *Fifth Business* the main character at first thinks he's the hero of his own story, which he narrates to us. He is, in fact, a decorated war hero, so he could by rights consider himself to be the Hero with a capital 'H'; yet he discovers as he goes along that he may be anything but that. For one thing, he doesn't get the girl, his childhood sweetheart – his arch-rival does. As it happens he learns during the course of the story that far from being the main character of this drama he could be better described as 'fifth business', a theatrical term that describes a character whose role is to link the male and female leads and the male and female oppositional characters (the second leads). Without fifth business none of the other characters could complete the actions that they are engaged in, since fifth business connects them and relays important information that makes the action possible. Davies' character sees this and, with humility and grace, sees that this is his role in life. As such, it frees him and he no longer has to go forward and fight all the fights, thinking he's the main figure everyone has to rely upon. He can have faith in the way the action unfolds, and in where it's going.

I mention this because, in some ways, we all have a tendency to do this. We want to see ourselves as the most important figure. Yet our real value may not be to stand in the glare of the footlights; it may be that we are destined to be part of something else entirely. Consider your life story that way, and see where it takes you.

If, for example, you had an abusive childhood you can choose to see your present situation as, perhaps, the triumphant conquering of that situation and the achievement of happiness, and that is certainly an heroic tale. It is a worthy life task and not an easy one, either. Yet it might also be that your role was to be able to break away from the source of the abuse so that you could give your children a better life than they might otherwise have had, a life fuelled by your understanding and love. Or it may be that on your way to clarity and peace you found your significant other, and that this caused you to have a more vital and productive life than would have been possible if you hadn't done the deep soul work you had to do. In this instance it may be that your soul work actually has created circumstances in which your partner is able to do something truly exceptional, something that eclipses your own public profile. It would be a mistake to see this as in any way a failing, but at the same time it takes an alert person to be able to move beyond the ego and the wish for praise. Think of the wise words of John the Baptist, who knew what he was doing but freely admitted that there would come a more important person than himself, one whose shoes he was not fit to tie, who would baptize with the Holy Spirit and not just with water. This was not humility and it certainly wasn't posing. It was real wisdom.

Take a moment, now, to think of yourself as a person who may have been a minor, but vital, character in the flow of life around you. Some people try to manufacture that status, of course, by setting their friends up on dates, for example, and then claiming praise if the outcome is successfully romantic. We're talking about something less obvious than this.

Hermann Hesse's novel *Knulp* gives us a good insight here. Knulp is a tramp and a scrounger, but he is sweet and honest for all that, and the novella ends with him dying of cold in a snowdrift. As he dies he thinks about whether he has wasted his life by following his calling as a tramp. A voice, perhaps from heaven, tells him that his purpose in life was to show others, hard-working peasants and farmers, that his way of life was not contemptible. They'd all envied him in his freedom, and they'd all pitied him too, and so they'd been able to go back to their ordinary tasks. They had honored the temporary desire to escape, and then returned to their life of toil, choosing that freely rather than seeing themselves as trapped. Without Knulp there would have been more discontent in the world he inhabited; without Knulp there would have been less possibility for spontaneous generosity of spirit and sharing. The villagers looked forward to his arrival and saved odd bits of clothing and food for him. He made them aware of how blessed their lives were, because they had more than enough compared to him. Knulp helped people to be kinder to each other because they were able to be kind to him. Which of us wouldn't be proud to have had such an effect on the people around us? Both Hesse and Robertson Davies were deep thinkers and both were followers of Jung. They saw that, perhaps, there is a Collective Unconscious, a world spirit that we are all a part of, and that seeing ourselves in this way is to notice that we exist in a pattern that may be constructed by some force that exists between human beings, even though they don't truly know it. We could call it God, or Fate, or anything we wish, but it certainly existed for these writers and for many others too. It's hard to see it because we are often so caught up in self-love. And possibly that is the task of any memoir writer: to use the memoir not to increase self-love but to try to move beyond it.

There are many ways to shape the memories you have collected so that you can begin to make sense of them. As we've already noted, people make experience coherent by breaking the flow of lived time into chunks, which then are constructed as stories. These stories need a beginning, a middle and end at the very least. This is a thoroughly artificial way of doing things, of course, because 'beginning' is a very fluid concept, just as 'end' is. The beginning of my life story could be just about anywhere, since I could argue that in order to understand my life we'd need to consider my mother, and in order to comprehend her we'd have to look at my grandparents, and so on. At the other end of the measure, when I die (which I won't be able to write about because I'll be rather too busy facing my extinction) my story probably won't be over because I'll have had an effect on many people, for good or ill, and they'll still be around to comment on me... But story making is how we, as human creatures, attempt to make sense of experience.

This tells us something important, therefore: stories are pulled out of the flow of time because they seem to express something we can't pin down any other way. Stay with this thought, because it suggests that every strong memory, every single one without exception, exists because something in our Unconscious has taken a chunk of time, isolated it (to some extent) from the rest of experience, and held onto it specifically because it has meaning – even if we don't consciously know what that meaning is yet. The soul, or the Unconscious if you prefer, has already chosen a series of small stories for us. And the soul has a sense of coherence all its own.

If we are to access these 'soul stories' we may need to let go of what the conscious self would like us to include. This part of our mind would like to have us include such things as the event of our first triumph and our first heartbreak, because these are surely important events. And indeed they may be. The question is whether you as a writer are going to focus on the things that are obvious or on the things that are rich with wisdom. Again, Vladimir Nabokov's memoir *Speak, Memory* is an example of this type of wisdom writing. In it he refers hardly at all to many of the things we, as readers, would presumably like to know about the great writer – when the books were composed, and how, and what he felt about his writing. He doesn't give us that. But he does give us vignettes that have a haunting quality I find very hard to pin down, and that clearly haunted him, too. His book is an examination of how memory works for him – and it's not a book in which he writes what he thinks the readers want to hear.

Here's another example that may help to show what I mean by soul stories. When my grandfather died he left me a few things including his watch. I'd never actually seen him wear the watch, which was very neat but somehow didn't interest me that much, so I placed it in a drawer. When we were clearing out his house, though, the other relatives divided up his presentation plaques, his silver trophies and so on, and I got his old penknife. That old penknife appealed to me more than anything else because he'd actually used it and carried it around with him for years, to the shooting competitions at which he'd won the trophies, for example. It therefore spoke to me more than the awards he'd been given (which had been chosen by others as being suitable presentation items) and it kept the man before me, rather than the man's resumé of achievements.

If I were to write something about my grandfather I'd probably start right there with his penknife. It conjures up a scene to me every time I look at it. It's one of those significant details I talked about earlier, something that's waiting to give its contribution to the story.

So, as you consider your life story I'd like you to select some objects, or some memories, and tell yourself 'think in scenes'. Think like a movie director. Each memory you have will be to some extent a visual one. Cherish those scenes. Draw up a list. As you do so more memories will come back. Discard nothing. Keep adding to the list.

When you have a series of scenes – and you need not try to connect them yet – try to recall them in as much detail as possible. What things looked like, felt like, smelled like, tasted of, and sounded like. What tone of voice did people have? Did their clothes feel rough or smooth? Perhaps you have particular perfumes associated with them? I bet you do.

Now, the point I'd like to make here is that each scene you pull from your memories is there for a reason. Memory researchers have known for some time now that we remember what seems valuable to us, even if we're not sure what the value is any more. Memories that have no resonance fade away forever. So you could say that every memory we are capable of retrieving carries a weight of importance that we, in our unconscious actions, have chosen to preserve – because it contains meaning. I think we've all experienced this. In classes I've witnessed students recall a memory and then say things like 'Now I see why my mother always put those pieces of string in that jar! It was because during the war there was a shortage of string for tying the fabric tops on homemade jams ...' On another occasion, as one man wrote the story of his life, he began to see how his uncle, who had been a figure of some importance to him, had become more and more restless and violent, and the writer hadn't been able to see why this might have been until he began to write his memories of small incidents. I've done it myself, recognizing that of course my father saved odds and ends of junk in his garage because, as a World War Two prisoner of war he had to save every little thing just to get by. His crammed garage, full of carefully labeled tins of old screws and washers and junk was, in fact, an expression of an old psychic wound. He finally got to have a place where he could put all those odds and ends he felt he just couldn't throw out. When he died and I had to clear the garage, I just couldn't throw those things out either.

The details can yield treasures.

If we take that example of my father we could add to it and say that I learned from him habits of frugality that still perplex me and make the rest of my family laugh. His salvaged tobacco tins of nuts and bolts expressed his inner landscape, one that gradually became my way of thinking and which I have since struggled to shrug off. And yes, some of those tins of my father's came back with me on the plane, weighing down my luggage so that the handle broke off one case when I carried it to the taxi. Which scene would I write? Would it be the one where I watch my father carefully put the tins on the shelf in order? Would it be the scene of the handle coming off my bag? Or perhaps it might turn out to be me watching my father root through the tins, find exactly what he was looking for, and make me a small model of a canon from wire and tubing, a model that was in that unfortunate suitcase and which now sits on my shelf of Treasures where I see it every day and am reminded of that event – of all those events. If we break this down we could say that the toy canon reminds me of several things: his wartime

experiences; his love for me; his tendency to hoard odds and ends; his inventiveness and dexterity; the lack of family funds for toys; his delight that he could do
something for me; his military background (it never occurred to him that model
guns wouldn't be suitable toys); his sense of order; and perhaps, behind all this,
his sense of accomplishment in any small manual task that he could undertake on
his own, which was perhaps linked to his feeling that in his military life there was
little scope for inventiveness. And yet, I'm aware of another aspect, which was that
the piece of tubing he used for the main part of the canon was a piece of piping I
had found and that I routinely used to look through, holding it up to my eye. My
father was anxious that I might poke it into my eye, since I was so fond of gazing
through it. His highly imaginative solution was to turn one toy into another, one
that I would not bring so dangerously close to either eye. And it worked. I was
happy, and my eyes were out of danger. One object, at least ten meanings, and
that's not even counting what I thought of the finished toy! Obviously I *felt* it was
important, although at age six I didn't know why, and in fact I had not analyzed
it in this way until just now, writing this. I just knew that I really valued it as an
ornament on my shelf. You may think this is way more than you need to know
about my family, but I wrote it because it's a strong example, one that grew as I
began writing it, and so it served its purpose even better than I realized when it
first sprang to mind. Writing, you see, brings meanings forward for all of us.

Doing soul work means finding the memories and then letting them tell you
their meaning.

In Hollywood they put things more forcefully. They say a script must have
conflict in every scene, or it'll be cut. This makes for exciting movies, which trans-
lates into money at the box office. We can also take this information and use it for
our soul work. Every memory, I suggest, already contains some sort of conflict,
however slight, and sometimes the slight, delicate conflicts are the most difficult
to deal with. The woman we mentioned earlier who recalled her mother's string
collecting clearly was deeply irritated by that habit. What she had to do was move
beyond thinking her mother was old-fashioned and silly and start to consider
that the irritation had something to do with her own impatience. Digging a little
more she was able to say that the string reminded her of her mother's depressive
worldview, which was a view she, the writer, had herself accepted for many years
and still wrestled with. She could have written the episode of the string and made
it comic – how silly her mother was! She could have written it as tragedy – how
limited her mother was! Or she could have taken the route she eventually did
which was to say, this is really about me and how like my mother I still am. That
last view was the start of soul work.

Perhaps a comparison here might help, and in this case I'll draw it from the visual arts. An accomplished artist, Kaetlyn Wilcox, described the process of creating her pictures in these terms: "It's important to me that when I begin a painting I have no idea how it will turn out." She says this in her artist's statement, and I'd like to point out the openness of that declaration. She then goes on to say how she explores her work at first.

> I like to make little drawings…. I keep all of these drawings, tacking them up or stowing them away…. Every other month or so I gather all of these loose bits in my studio and play with them, challenging myself to turn them into *something*…. I add bits here and there, drawing, painting, and sewing, until a new story emerges.

This is the visual equivalent of what we've been exploring. Even though Kaetlyn Wilcox's statement is not the final word on this matter, it is certainly representative of the way many artists and writers work, and it depicts what is an essential aspect of memoir writing. In these pages I've asked you to do something very similar. I've asked you to generate new material without attempting to put it into any sort of order, at least to begin with. Then there will come a time when it feels appropriate to gather the scenes and see what they tell you. Notice, though, it only works for Kaetlyn, as she says, if she doesn't know how things will turn out in advance. As writers we too have to try and refrain from coming to the premature closure that shuts off possibilities.

So, to recap: think in scenes. Then be aware that every scene involves a conflict and the conflict might not be the one you think. It may not be just between you and your parent, for instance. It may also be between you and the values you have internalized from that parent – values that you do not want to hold on to – in which case the conflict exists within you.

For some people, of course, a life story will be filled with conflict, sometimes violent conflict of a truly frightening sort. It may be very hard to write such scenes. If that is the case, you don't have to do it. If, when you were five, your father beat up your mother in front of your eyes and then deserted the family, that is a major event. You should probably write something about it for your own psychic health. But you do not have to dwell on it nor do you have to give it more space than anything else. For it just might be that your father's actions were horrible, but they gave rise to something richer and better. Perhaps you became closer to your mother as a direct result. Perhaps you were relieved that your father had finally left. The real focus, then, would be on the way the relationship with your mother was able to change and grow. Hollywood would probably focus on the violence because it makes for riveting cinema. I'd suggest that there's not much wisdom to be learned from violence and so focusing on it might be a mistake.

Here I have to offer a word of caution, which is that if you have had traumatic violence in your life you may well need to enlist the help of a professional counselor to guide you through the process of recovery. Writing could well be an important component of this process, and some people can write their way to health. But certainly not all people can do it alone. Severe trauma is like a traffic accident: you'll need help and medical personnel until you've been stabilized. When you're feeling better you may need the gentler, longer term healing of writing. If you elect to work with a counselor, then I'd urge you to write about each session and your reactions to it, and perhaps to keep a diary through the days between sessions. This may well turn out to be a part of the soul work you need to do and, as I have witnessed, it most certainly can become a memoir in its own right. Mary Lou Shields' memoir *Sea Run* is about exactly this process.

The important thing to recall in all of this is that we tend to select the stories about ourselves and, having selected, we believe the stories to be true – whether or not they actually are. One could write a memoir about oneself that focused only on the dramatic or the tragic, and that might well make for breath-taking reading and enormous sales. To do so one only has to zero in on the dramatic parts of one's life. We all have them and we can all make them seem more dramatic if we so wish. Almost everyone who has stepped outside their front door has met with episodes that include death, danger, ruthless people, and incredible kindness, too. But it's not what you can make your story into that matters, it's what actually feels true, because whatever story you tell will be making you, *you.*

In some texts intended to guide you through the memoir process, you'll read about how to make your life story have a rhythm and have various climaxes just like a well-constructed novel – and one must be wary of this simply because it's playing to the gallery. It's easy to do, and it probably won't get you anywhere your soul needs to go. We all have far too much experience of self-justification already, so refuse the temptation to write for revenge, or for what you think justice might be. You can choose something better. You can write for understanding.

So, if you have a scene that you recall, or perhaps that you've already written from your point of view, try writing it from the point of view of the antagonist. If it's about an argument with a sibling or a spouse, try writing it from that other person's viewpoint. This won't always be comfortable, but it just might be necessary.

In this section I've asked you to think of your life in terms of scenes, since that is how your Unconscious has already divided up your experience. I've also asked you to consider that in each scene there will be a gem, hidden in the conflict that is inevitably present. When you have enough of these scenes you will, quite simply, begin to perceive a new shape to your life story. You may look at it and say, as one of my writers did, "Wow, my life went through several big alterations, and each time it did so I found myself saying goodbye to one dog and getting another. During a neurotic period of my life I had a neurotic dog, and when she died, I got a lazy dog and I was more laid back. And then I got this intelligent little mutt and, bang, my life changed again…." This woman came to the conclusion that the dogs she'd owned had picked up on the energy in her life, and so they'd been mirrors, of a sort. And suddenly she had a structure for the memoir she knew she wanted to write – about how she'd found her way to stability despite a very unstable home life in which she felt dogs were about the only creatures she could trust.

Structure is not always what you think it might be.

Here are some exercises that may help you to think creatively about structure. Write the story of your shoes. Write the story, with photographs if you have them, of your haircuts, or your hats. Write the story of your cars.

These prompts can provide a great deal of fun when done individually or in groups. They can also be extremely revealing. Shoes may not sound like an important topic, but when we're young our shoes are chosen for us at time when we have very little choice about anything, and they may please us or quite the opposite. Writers have brought up memories of uncomfortable shoes, of worn out shoes, of their favorite shoes that they couldn't bear to part with… and each memory has produced a new insight. Were you made to wear shoes that were practical but not stylish? Was there a measure of social embarrassment?

Shoes are capable of providing visceral responses. They are the thing that keeps you from the worst of the elements, mud and snow and rain. In a good pair of shoes we all feel better about ourselves, and about the world. Often writers will produce memories of the first time they bought shoes using their own money, and how that felt like a moment of independence that could hardly be overstated. Sometimes people have produced stories of having to carry their 'good shoes' to the place they were headed, and then change out of galoshes or less stylish items. One man wrote about how he had looked for years for a set of cowboy boots that he thought would be so cool, only to find when he had a pair, which were exactly what he wanted, they weren't really very comfortable to walk in. They sat in his closet for another ten years, practically unused, a mute reproach to his idealism and deferred gratification. As he wrote about them he came to the soul work he needed to complete. The boots were about what looked good rather than what was actually useful, he decided, and he made a resolution to reassess his life in terms of what actually worked and gave him what he needed, so he could let go of the things he thought he 'ought' to need but didn't, and the things he thought he couldn't throw out because they represented so much of his past longing, his invested time. For him the shoes exercise became about getting unstuck in his life.

He also wrote some hilarious pieces about other shoes he'd owned.

This is not very different from such pieces as Kyoko Mori's short essay/memoir about knitting, appropriately called *Yarn*, in which she circles around the history of knitting, then explains her own pleasure in knitting, and finally she brings the reader to the point at which she hints that knitted clothing, objects that are shaped to life needs, provide the knitter with great comfort because one can always undo the pattern and remake it correctly – something that's hard to do in life, and seductively easy to do in memoir.... Memoirs proceed one word at a time, just as knitting moves forward, one knot after another, linear but woven together, one thread but many. It's a beguiling metaphor.

The history of the cars one has owned can be similarly rich. One's first car is hard to forget, especially if one went out and haggled for it oneself, and then had to pay for it when it broke down, or rusted out, or blew a radiator hose on a desert highway in Mexico. What we find, of course, is that it's also the history of how well we decide to treat ourselves with the resources at our disposal. As such it says a great deal about our spiritual level of awareness. Men, particularly, have sometimes gone on to write about vehicles they've restored and made beautiful – and in some ways the restoration process has been about the attempt to put some aspect of life in order, and then, as they've ridden in the car, to live that orderliness. Obviously it can become more complex than this. Or as therapist Penny Jones phrased it, 'Vehicles can be a good vehicle for all sorts of things.'

I mention this specific exercise of writing about beloved (or much hated) cars because men find this extremely useful as a way into their life experiences, and men are frequently in the minority in my classes and workshops, sometimes feeling they have no voice at all and no right to comment upon their lives. The trick is to keep the focus off the details of the carburetor and *on* the values that were mutely articulated by the car or motorcycle as a whole. One can shape an entire memoir around such concrete items. Take a look at Fred Haefele's story of restoring his Indian motorcycle, *Rebuilding the Indian; A Memoir* (2005) to see what I mean. As he rebuilds the motorcycle he also rebuilds his sense of himself and what his life could be.

Notes

1. Deepak Chopra, speaking at the New York Ethical Society on July 17, 2008.
2. Robertson Davies, *Fifth Business*, Penguin, (reprint) 2001.
3. John the Baptist, *Matthew* 3, 11: 'but he that cometh after me is mightier than 1, whose shoes I am not worthy to bear.' This is echoed in *Luke* 3, 16-17, 'the latchet of whose shoes I am not worthy to unloose.'
4. Hermann Hesse, *Knulp*, Suhrkamp, 1962.
5. Vladimir Nabokov, op. cit.

6. Kaetlyn Wilcox, Artist's Statement (2008). This statement and her work can be seen at http://web.mac.com/kaetlynwilcox/iweb/site/Home.html
7. Mary Lou Shields, *Sea Run; Surviving My Mother's Madness*, Seaview Books, 1981.
8. Kyoko Mori, *Yarn*, in *Harvard Review*, 24, 2003; later reprinted in *Best American Essays 2004*, Houghton Mifflin, 2004.
9. Penny Jones, Consulting Therapist, Peper Harow Foundation, private conversation, 1985.
10. Fred Haefele, *Rebuilding the Indian: A Memoir*, Bison Books, (2005)

Chapter Thirteen

Details, Details, Details... Research and How to Use It

How much detail should you put in? That's the question that often comes up in workshops, so I'd like to answer it in a round about way, as there can be no definitive answer. A man in one group was writing about the life of his grandmother who had been taken to Auschwitz in 1942 and had died there. He'd done huge amounts of painstaking research. He'd been able to uncover the Nazi records that showed the precise time of departure of the train on which she and some of her children had been loaded, their arrest numbers, the time the train arrived at Auschwitz, their subsequent prison numbers and so on. It was a mass of detail that clearly held a horrifying fascination. Unfortunately the writing was dull. The man himself was close to tears as he shared his piece, but somehow the room was feeling *his* pain, but not the pain of the event. If we'd simply read the account by ourselves I think the numbers would have overwhelmed us.

As a piece of self-expression this man had done something that meant a great deal to him. But as communication it hadn't worked. I thought about his approach and decided 'too much detail'. Then, a few hours later I realized what the problem might be – too little detail, or rather an overload of only one kind of detail. What he'd described to us was the inhuman precision of the Nazi transportation arrangements that kept such meticulous records about something so ghastly. What he hadn't done was to give any human details that would allow us, or him, to see the event in a context that would reveal something new. To be told horrors is unpleasant, but it doesn't bring forward understanding. For example, he'd mentioned that his grandmother had been loaded into a cattle truck. This sounds bad, and I've no doubt it was very bad indeed. It might have been useful for him to research accounts written by survivors in order to find out what it actually felt like, smelt like, to be on those trucks for several days. The material could have been introduced without violating the flow of his story, and would perhaps have strengthened the emotional impact. Sensory details, however, were missing.

And here's another thought. It seems the cattle trucks were painted with signs that said '8 horses or 40 men' in German, yet over a hundred people were crammed in to each. Now, that alone is horrifying. As it stands it's a strong statement; but I'd also argue that here was a detail that begged for some interpretation. Today we don't think traveling in a cattle truck is a humane way to treat people, although I've certainly traveled in trains in the Far East that come close. The trucks to Auschwitz were designed to hold 40 soldiers, and their equipment, and were considered quite adequate for enlisted men at the time. Indeed, the trucks had no seats so it was easy for the soldiers to lie down and sleep. This sort of truck was standard transport, which is one reason that in many cases the victims didn't immediately panic or fight back. What was not standard treatment was the overcrowding, the total lack of sanitary facilities, the mixture of old and young, men and women, sick and healthy, the complete absence of any food, and the tendency not to allow the doors to be opened at any time. In fact the punctilious railway officials probably would have obeyed the '40 men' rule if they'd had enough trucks, but this was wartime and they were beset by shortages. In their minds this was most likely seen as a reasonable way to solve a problem *as far as they were concerned*. Suddenly, if we wish to see it, we have some insight into the minds that could, little by little, have reconciled themselves to perpetrating such a horror. They had to have ways to rationalize away the actuality of what they were doing - mental escape clauses, as it were - and that insight is worth considering.

This is a long example, but I use it because the mass of detail the man had gathered about the last train-ride his grandmother made had, as its implicit text, the inquiry as to how human beings could do this to each other. That's a valuable question, and to some extent the answer was available to him if he'd chosen to see it. But he wanted only to be in a place of outrage and sorrow. Who could blame him? Unfortunately that sort of thinking tends to be rather black and white and, while it shows horrors, it does not seek to comprehend them. No one would disagree that the death camps are to be condemned. Soul work, however, may require something more. And that's where the questions begin. One that always pops up is why did these functionaries of the railways preserve such records, especially at a time when so much else was destroyed? I think if I'd been forced at gunpoint to be part of something like that I'd be very eager to destroy all traces! In a situation where there was so much destruction it would have been very easy, surely, to set fire to everything. But they didn't. In fact it seems as if these records were more carefully preserved than most at the time. What sort of mind does that? Was it fear? Was it a way to hang onto sanity as a whole civilization was being pounded to dust? We might never know, but it is psychologically interesting. Serving military men I have spoken with have kept records in a way that echoes this. One man kept a detailed account of how his aircraft was shot down, and preserved it for years in various prisons camps and, yes, while traveling on trains just like the one the grandmother was on, because, he said, "Someone, one day, would want to know what we'd done with their airplane." Was this a way of maintaining hope that there would in fact be a day, eventually, a day of peace when he'd be asked to account for what had happened? Perhaps that hope kept him sane. As it turns out no one ever did ask him.

In all this I am not trying to diminish the importance of the tale the man was telling about his grandmother. It was important and he'd worked hard. Yet it seemed to be an opportunity missed for understanding at a deeper level. The deeper level is what we are after. Those railway officials were not monsters, although they behaved in ways that brought about monstrous results. They were probably just like anyone, just like you and me, and yet they allowed themselves to be intimidated and manipulated. But they also manipulated their own minds so that they could get through each day without wishing to kill themselves in despair, and the evidence was right there. Now that's a real horror, too.

There are, of course, more ways today to explore and research than ever before. The Internet is a marvelous place and if one chooses carefully the information one can discover can be astounding. In terms of searching for relatives and Ellis Island records, there are not only public archives but also societies one can join that will help you trace your relatives. This is hardly news. What matters is what you do with this information – which is why I gave the example of the gentleman who had researched his grandmother's deportation to Auschwitz. You will, no matter what, have to interpret the information you have, and you'll have to use your imagination to make it come alive for you so it can be felt. This requires taking a risk. You may imagine a situation and you may imagine it in a way that is the complete opposite of what it was. You may imagine the grandmother consoling the children by telling nursery stories, or you may imagine her slumped in despair, depending upon what you feel she might have been most likely to do. In each case you'll probably be writing about what you want and need her to have been: you'll be projecting you. There's nothing wrong with that. In fact it's an important part of soul work if you admit it. One way to do so is to write about it knowing that this is the image you want. "I'd like to think of her, sitting on the filthy straw as if it were the most natural thing in the world for a woman of 45 in her best dress, a child nestled against each shoulder, as she told the story of Snow White...." By writing it like that you will give yourself the image of a strong ancestor, one you can be proud of – and that may be what you need. If so, then acknowledge it, and your writing will remain true to who you are. For memoir writing is seeking your truth.

This leads us to a different, but linked, discussion about the use of detail. One thing that I ask writers to watch out for in their own work and in the work of others is the use of cliché. We all do it, as a sort of shorthand if we're rushed. Occasionally, though, cliché and jargon can conceal important information. When a policeman says he 'restrained' a prisoner, what does that mean? Did he put a firm hand on his shoulder and tell him to calm down? Or did he sit on him and tie his hands and ankles together behind his back in the classic hog-tie? There is a difference. When a writer describes a person as 'plump and sixty' that is so sketchy that we're tempted to ask some questions. Is the description so vague because there is only a vague memory of the person? Or is the description as it is because this person was so familiar, seen so often, that the writer has stopped noticing fully who he or she actually is? If the second case is true, then this represents an opportunity! We tend to stop truly seeing those people who are around us every day – and so we tend to minimize their effect on our lives.

One woman wrote about her courtship and marriage as "like a fairy tale", and even though she meant that to stand in contrast to what happened later in the narrative, which was anything but a fairy tale, it somehow suggested an unrealistic grasp on the situation that I urged her to explore. Had she been dazzled? What was she expecting married life to be? What had she been told? And who had told her? It was when she began to look behind the phrase that she saw how she'd developed ideas that were an interesting mixture of pure idealism and healthy realism. The cliché had not allowed her to know that, fully.

Another writer on one occasion described a relative as domineering and controlling, and left it at that. Since the person concerned had been the father of one of the main participants in the story it felt too important to by-pass. When she began to describe this man by saying he'd climbed the tallest mountain in the Swiss Alps twice (in the days when mountain climbing was in its early development), that he'd run his own business empire producing supplies for sewing machines and had later branched out into the manufacturing of the machines themselves – that was when a more vital picture began to emerge. Again, the details matter; but notice, it's not just any details that we're discussing here. It is always a case of choosing the details that show a character or situation in a more forceful light. The detail in this case had been a lump of rock – from a peak of the Alps – that this man always used as a paperweight on his desk. Immediately it gives us a sense of who he might have been, even if it's not spelled out to us.

Cliché can also be a way of disguising things from ourselves. When a soldier writes that he neutralized a position, it means that he killed everyone there and surely that will be an event that deserves to be considered in some detail, if he can bear it. Sometimes writers in this position cannot bear to think about the facts behind the cliché, and that has to be respected if soul work is to happen. Yet it also has to be noted, so the event is not bypassed. In my father's memoir, for example, he describes how he returned from four years as a prisoner of war and as he walked down the street there was a banner saying welcome, and a homecoming "such as anyone could have wished for". After he was dead my aunt told a different story. There was no banner because no one knew when he'd be coming back – or if he'd be coming back. When he walked into the house the only person home was his father, sitting by the fire. It seems that my father (who didn't get on that well with his father) came in and asked how everyone was. He was then told his younger brother had been killed in action, and that they hadn't written to tell him because they didn't want to worry him. At this my father turned around, walked right out of the house leaving all the doors open, and didn't come back until very late that night. Now, one can see why he might have chosen not to write about that. Instead he covered it with a well-worn phrase and a familiar image – the happy homecoming. Yet I can't help thinking that the actuality might have been the richer experience for the reader and certainly would have been a place where the writer could have done some soul work. For, by using the cliché, it was clear he was still angry with his family, all those years later. It was a missed opportunity for some soul work and some forgiveness.

So where does this leave us? Clearly, detail is very near the center of memoir and since what we remember in the heat of the moment has significance we can rarely understand at the time, we need to recall the event in as much detail as possible so we can ask questions about it later. The woman who recalled seeing her aunt hit by a car remembered that the aunt "flew high in the air, higher than the houses". In actual fact she knew the aunt had not been propelled that high, but as a small child who had been, moments before, holding the aunt's hand it might have seemed like it. Who but a child could have thought like that? In recapturing the moment she recaptured the emotion and the viewpoint – and to some extent let the reader feel how such things can haunt a child long into adulthood. What's important here is not my clumsy, wordy exposition, but her awareness of her way of seeing the event, simultaneously as the child experienced it then and as the grown woman can understand it now. Memoir exists, to some extent, always in a sort of double-focus. We feel the moment as it was, yet we know we're alive now in a different time, observing. Choosing the right detail makes it possible to recreate the event.

Chapter Fourteen

Overlooked and Hidden Memories: The Lies We Tell Ourselves

I'd like to try another exercise with you now, which may help to break loose those memories we habitually overlook. For the best results you will need a partner to help you, but if you don't have one you can do it by email with a friend, and if you have no one you care to work with you can still benefit from it. Sometimes the best way to proceed in group work is to match people up with those they don't know very well. This works better, for the most part, than choosing a friend.

I'd like you to think about an event in your life, about something that you did or said, which you feel you can be proud of. It has to be your own doing – feeling pride in a son or daughter will not be sufficient here. Now, with your partner, sit facing each other, preferably on similar chairs. Decide who will go first and that person will have exactly two minutes, timed, to speak about the event of which he or she is proud, and how it felt. During this time the listener may not speak or write, but must focus on the speaker. At the end of two minutes, pause. Don't say anything for thirty seconds. Then the listener has a minute and a half to repeat back everything he can recall. After that is completed, the original speaker gets to correct any mistakes. Now, take a five-minute break and make a few notes on what happened and how the exercise felt. Then do the same thing again, with the roles reversed. Keep to the rules of time, and of who gets to speak when, or the exercise won't work.

At the end, take a few minutes to write down your reactions.

Too often we do things well and yet we feel we cannot share them with others because that's not socially acceptable, or it's perceived as boasting. In this way we forget to remind ourselves of our successes and we forget to make ourselves aware of our effectiveness. If we routinely ignore our successes, eventually we begin to feel we have nothing to be proud of. This has the effect of removing us from our courage, of draining from us a vital source of energy. And it is our courage we must honor if we are to see ourselves fully, because we're going to need it as we write. Consider for a moment: the Army is very good at this since it permits soldiers to wear and display their medal ribbons – their successes – all the time. As such they feel, and are, more effective in what they do. They are able to access their own strength of will more readily, and if they can't do it easily they have regimental badges to remind them of the honors of the unit. Unfortunately our culture doesn't have similar public ways of honoring our courage and successes outside the military. When you write your memoir you'll have to come to terms with what you did well – not just with the things that turned out badly. Goodness knows those are hard enough to write about, but for some reason acknowledging our successes is harder for many people.

People who have done this exercise have reported several things, perhaps the first of which is that they are surprised to be in a situation where another is really listening to them, paying attention. For many of us *being heard* is an unusual experience, almost as unfamiliar as really listening to others. When we recognize this we learn just how unaccustomed we all are to paying attention to what is actually being said. As a result, we stop saying very much ourselves. This may not sound like news, yet if we don't acknowledge that this happens we can become blind to the ways we will tend to censor ourselves in a memoir. It's also much more socially acceptable to focus on our failures than to point out what we did right. In this way we de-skill ourselves.

A moment to be proud of, after all, doesn't have to be very large. Not many people win national prizes. But it may just be that at one point, in a tricky situation, we did exactly the right thing, in precisely the right way. We knew the right words to defuse a situation. We spoke from our hearts and not from our pride, and changed the way things unfolded later.

This is a little touch of the Magician, and it will wither away if it isn't recognized, encouraged and nurtured. It's the realm of inspiration, too. You will need to have such moments of inspiration in your memoir, and once you start looking for them they'll be everywhere.

Once, when leading this exercise, there was a woman who could not think of anything she was proud of – nothing at all. This became the start of a deeper exploration in which she was able to see how her 'nice lady' persona was cutting her off from any sense of being authentic, and so was actively silencing her voice in her memoir. It was high time to break through this self-imposed silence. So, what are the things you are silent about? Who are the people you feel shut you down in this way? These will be important considerations.

If we see what we did right we'll not ignore the things we didn't do correctly, and we certainly won't be overlooking the bad things that happened in our lives. Instead we'll be seeing ourselves as directors and shapers of our lives, to some extent, and we'll balance up any tendency we might have to see ourselves as victims. I think you can see how useful this can be. After you've done the exercise find some more moments you are proud of. They might prove valuable.

Here's a different exercise that may be useful for you as you take on your memoir. Read the following poem. Now try reading it out loud. Perhaps you already know it. It's a famous nonsense poem by Lewis Carroll.

> 'Twas brillig and the slithy toves
> Did gyre and wimble in the wabe,
> All mimsy were the borogoves,
> And the mome raths outgrabe.

> "Beware the Jabberwock, my son,
> The jaws that bite, the claws that catch.
> Beware the Jubjub bird and shun
> The frumious bandersnatch."

> He took his vorpal blade in hand,
> Long time the manxome foe he sought,
> So rested he by the Tumtum tree,
> And stood awhile in thought.

> And as in uffish thought he stood,
> The Jabberwock, with eyes of flame,
> Came whiffling through the tulgey wood,
> And burbled as it came!

> One-two, One-two, and through and through
> The vorpal blade went snicker-snack.
> He left it dead, and with its head,
> He went galumphing back.

> "And hast thou slain the Jabberwock?
> Come to my arms my beamish boy!
> Oh frabjous day, Calloo, Callay!"
> He chortled in his joy.

> 'Twas brillig and the slithy toves
> Did gyre and gimble in the wabe,
> All mimsy were the borogoves,
> And the mome raths outgrabe.

Try out some of those words. What could they mean? The main thrust of the poem is fairly clear, if you look at it. A Jabberwock with 'eyes of flame' is in a wood, and seems to be killed by a boy – at least as far as we can tell.

What I'd like you to do now is to imagine what a Jabberwock might look like. Take a moment or two to visualize it. Close your eyes. It seems to be some kind of monster with its 'claws that catch'. Can you see it? If so, then I'd like you to draw one. What kind of creature is it? If you're not good at drawing then you can label things on your diagram, but try drawing, just for now, anyway.

I've done this exercise with writers for some years now; in fact I first mentioned it in my book *The Sanity Manual* back in 1995. Each time we do this drawing I learn more, and the people I'm with do too.

On one occasion I asked a workshop of people to do this exercise and the young woman to my left pulled out a pen, gripped it in her fist, and drew a stick figure with such force that she almost ripped the paper. Everyone in the room could hear the sound of her pen tip scoring the page. She slapped her pen down on the table and glared around, defiantly, finished after forty five seconds. Everyone else in the room was working away quietly. Receiving no reaction she noisily pulled out a magazine and began to read, ostentatiously flipping the pages. It was quite a show. The remainder of the people continued to work away. It was utterly silent in the room for over twenty minutes and then many of the participants put down their pens and pencils and looked around, while a few continued working away for another ten minutes or so.

The somewhat melodramatic reaction by this young woman led me to ask her, first, how she had felt the exercise had been, since she had finished first. She was obviously very angry, glowered at me and said, "Everybody knows I can't draw! Since I was four everyone's known that. So why did you ask me to draw?" My reply was that since I'd only just met her in this workshop, and since I knew nothing about her, I couldn't possibly have known about her life at the age of four, and that I was sorry to have been the cause of any distress. Since no one else in the room knew her either I was interested that she thought we all knew about her difficulties. The rawness of her reaction spelled out that in her family she had been shamed or ridiculed for her drawing, which had started at the age of four and, moreover, she knew this and yet still resented it violently almost twenty-five years later! The exercise had been an unwitting trigger for some deep rage. This – surely – was what she would have to explore in her soul work. Who had ridiculed her, and why, and why was it still so painful? This was her Jabberwock.

She was in some ways just a clear version of what many writers experience with this exercise. Some refuse to draw and write descriptions instead. Many moan and groan at the first mention of drawing; I always note that with interest, since this is not an art class and the object is not to create a beautiful picture. When this happens it's as well to realize that we're dealing with people who have suffered criticism for their draftsmanship and who have internalized that sense of being 'not good enough' to the extent that they still feel shame. Most people experience themselves as either good or bad at art only in about first grade. That's when we start accepting the world's view of what we do as the accurate one. At age three we'll happily play with crayons and paper all day, not caring whether the result is 'good' or not – and we'll proudly show the scribbling to Mom and expect to have the pages taped to the fridge for all to see. At its most basic this exercise can ask you to tap into that early time when you met an unkind world that disapproved of you, perhaps for the very first time.

Most people doing this exercise will just get on and create a drawing. When sketching in this way the Unconscious tends to be allowed out and it will create all sorts of useful images that are unpremeditated, and which bring pleasure. To see a room full of adults drawing monsters for half an hour, totally absorbed, is quite an experience. Some even say that they haven't had so much fun since grade school. Most haven't drawn anything for years, and are delighted that they still can. It can be a major rediscovery for some.

If the exercise works well what you may have created here is a sketch, a symbol, of the things that get in your way when you try to do your soul work. To that extent this will be a rendition of your very own private monster. In order to understand this fully we'll have to go over the drawings carefully, one step at a time.

In viewing your monster you may need to consider certain things, such as how much space on the page the creature takes up. A small drawing may indicate an unimportant concern, something that worries you just a little. A large drawing may indicate that there are things that are large right now in your life that you want to address. Remember, though, that this will be your perception, and it may only indicate your attitude to the concern, rather than its importance. The man who drew a small rat wrote about how it symbolized for him a small loan he had to pay off. What he didn't admit until later was that the 'loan' was one he'd taken from his company without permission. Conversely, the woman who drew a small cuddly creature crowded into a corner of a page was indicating that in her life she felt as if she was a cuddly, inoffensive person who regularly got crowded out of consideration, and even felt she had no room of her own in her own home.

Similarly, whether the creature is facing the viewer or looking off to one side may suggest how this problem seems, now. Is it 'in your face' or is it something that is not disturbing you right now? Those people who draw toothed creatures, whose roaring faces fill the whole page, may well be expressing a sense of a problem that is right before them, today.

The monsters that are drawn can be, and often are, just about everything imaginable. How big was your creature in real terms – bigger than you? Is it male or female or neither? How does it threaten you?

Many people report that the monster is male, and larger than they are, in which case there is a fairly good chance that it may represent a fear of a father figure or an authority (since males dominate our authority structures), but we must be aware here that the exercise can be many things for many people. Frequently I've had writers identify the monster as their fathers – and for them that may be true. Sometimes people are very excited about this, and they begin to speak about the tensions of living with their fathers or the miseries of having been abandoned by him. If that seems to be the case for you then this will be a major figure for you to deal with in your soul work. The drawing may provide significant clues as to what the issues are. The woman who drew a creature with dozens of mouths could hardly contain herself as she said that it was her mother, she'd just realized, and her mother was always talking and never listening. These are good direct responses and they indicate what the issues those writers have to face might be. Yet I'd point out that the drawing on the page is not, actually, your father (or mother, or uncle). It is, instead, the creature that comes into existence when you allow yourself to contact your feelings about your father and all those people who are in your eyes like your father. It is, in effect, a creature that symbolizes what gets in your way as you try to deal with this barrier to your soul work. This is a rendition of the creature that stops you going where you need to go. So you are going to have to know what it is, who it is, and how to deal with it. It's your own private monster, and you'd better work out how to make sure it doesn't take over your writing or silence you on important topics.

Women writers have often drawn diagrams of creatures that they describe as misunderstood, as essentially harmless, as unlucky or alienated, or as being kind on the inside. Many times these pictures are actually representations of themselves, since they feel themselves to be misunderstood and victimized because of it. Occasionally the pictures will have the boy in them, too, sometimes waiting to kill the monster. What emerges from this, for the most part, is a sense in the writers that they have been too nice and too forgiving of those who do not treat them properly. They feel stuck in the role of being 'nice' and that this has become monstrous for them, since it stops them asserting themselves and being who they want to be. Again, this is the creature that stops them going where they need to go in their soul work, and it will have to be dealt with - perhaps even killed off – so that they can get on with their personal growth.

To that extent, many of the pictures will be self-portraits in a codified form. The woman who drew a creature that was fading into the mist with one side of its face showing happiness and the other side tears was able to make a connection to her habitual behavior as a 'people pleaser' who always put her needs last and who was more than happy to become whatever it was others needed her to be. Her real feelings were smothered and she faded from notice. Obviously anyone who is engaged in a search for truth in a memoir is going to have to risk not pleasing everyone all the time, and it will also be a major life issue, as we can never please everyone in our daily lives either. The picture was a call to her to abandon an old way of being, one that left her not knowing what she was feeling, happiness or sadness.

One of the more dramatic episodes was of a man in his thirties who burst into a long tirade about how the old father had set up the young boy for an impossible task to kill the Jabberwock and the young boy has no choice but to go off into the woods and face the creature and it just wasn't fair! It was very hard to get a word in edgeways and, as he became more excited and spoke more loudly, he could not hear my words anyway. Finally he declared, 'That's what it means', stood up and ran out of the room. I never saw him again. Pretty obviously the exercise had brought up many difficult father issues, old resentments, betrayals, and a huge amount of fear. He'd named his issues, and his soul work. Yet it seemed he just couldn't face them right now.

I mention this because we need to acknowledge that this is not an exercise for rainy Saturday afternoons when one is bored. At its best this exercise can turn anyone inside out – and we'd better be ready for what happens. That's why I've put it towards the end of this book. I used to use it early in my workshops as a way of breaking open the major issues right away, and some people couldn't manage it. In short, it panicked some writers and that was neither kind of me nor productive for them.

Our defenses run deep, after all, and we've all worked for years to perfect them, therefore we have to be compassionate as we dismantle them. So, for example, every so often I'll come across someone who draws a perfect Mickey Mouse, or a careful rendition of an action figure. Such meticulously rendered pictures can reveal clues, but the cultural values will be hard to chip through since the picture is supposed to look a certain, recognizable, way. The man who drew the cartoon figure he'd practiced every day of his life since he was ten was probably going to a 'safe' image that he knew he could produce which would also be relatively well drawn. So he was, in effect, hiding behind a product he thought others would admire instead of drawing what came into his imagination. Defensiveness is not a crime, but it's extremely valuable to know that this is what one will do in place of being authentic, if one is prepared to acknowledge that. Otherwise it's just another defense. Knowing what our defenses are will help us to leave them behind.

The actions shown on the page can also offer openings for the soul worker. The woman who drew a monster hiding behind trees peeping at her, was able to show it as a dramatization of the anorexia that had 'stalked' her (her word) for years. Similarly, the man who drew an empty landscape and indicated that the Jabberwock was underground was able to go on and write about how he buried his emotions. The older man who drew a beautiful horse rearing on its hind legs while small figures stabbed at it with knives, found he had drawn himself surrounded by his three older brothers, with whom he had considerable friction.

This exercise has had as many variant responses as there are people. I have never had two monsters exactly the same, although I have seen many that are somewhat similar. Once you have drawn your Jabberwock you won't simply have drawn a creature that you're afraid of. You'll have created a picture of something that until now may have been shapeless inside you. Now it exists, it has been 'named' in that process, and you can see how to deal with it. Will you need help to confront this creature? If so, who will you recruit? Perhaps by doing the exercise you'll have realized that everyone has an issue to stare down, and that this is part of the task of memoir. From this you'll know you're not alone. Others have gone down this road before you, and they are with you in spirit, and you can draw strength from that.

My own Jabberwock, for years, appeared always with a long neck. It wasn't until I'd thought about it for a while that I realized that the creature simply could not be fought head-on. It was just too big. Instead I'd need to attack from the side and slice that vulnerable neck. In terms of life advice this was invaluable. I could see that confrontation, which I tended to favor at the time, would get me nowhere, but that if I waited I would get my opening. In a sense that's what this exercise is, too. It encourages you to go towards a drawing task, while the real material will have to be approached at an angle, when the defenses are down, or at least pointed in another direction. Drawing does that. The conscious mind says 'Oh, this is just a silly drawing. I can relax', and when it does that it lets down its defenses and the Unconscious can flow more freely.

The exercises in this chapter have both been about the forces that will keep you silent and fearful if you do not acknowledge them. They have also shown us, to some extent, the unarticulated messages we carry within us about who we are. Being polite and not recognizing our achievements may be socially accepted, but it's also a defense that stops us having to know the full extent of who we are. Not thinking about that monster that keeps us silent can be a way of not allowing ourselves to step forward so we don't have to act, and this too can be a defense. We now have no further use for these defenses, and can let them go. Independent of the memoir these are valuable life lessons. If the exercises have worked properly we'll have uncovered these lies we carry in our souls; and it's time to get rid of them.

Notes

1. Lewis Carroll's Jabberwocky originally appeared in *Through The Looking Glass, and What Alice found There*, 1872.
2. Allan Hunter, *The Sanity Manual*, Kroshka Books, New York, 1998, p. 22.

Chapter Fifteen

The Six Stages as Mirrored in this Book

B y now you may have noticed that the exercises I've offered also form a pattern. The first exercises were about you as a child, an Innocent in terms of the archetypes, who is facing the sense of being an Orphan. The aim was to help you to remember, and also to reconnect with the energy of the authentic you before you became too socialized, dutiful, or perhaps rebellious and oppositional. Each reaction is a movement away from the authentic, centered, you. And it is that authentic person we will need to hold onto if we are to see what your soul can grow to become.

The exercises in which I asked you to produce a writing file, a Treasure Chest, and a Contract, were an invitation to a form of adoption, one that would create a productive working schedule. It was, in effect, a way to ensure that you could be in the Orphan stage without being disaffected or destructive. The intent was to introduce you to a way of gathering material, and also of suspending judgment about how that material should be used, as it's always so tempting to want to get on with the task of 'writing the memoir' and have a 'result'. The Orphan arche-type loves results that one can point to and be reassured by.

Of course, in all this the Pilgrim archetype is emerging as you find it possible, I hope, to explore your life and ask questions about it. Even asking basic questions about the structure of the memoir is a way of seeing the bigger picture, of asking what it all truly adds up to. And this is the work of the Pilgrim.

Perhaps just as important is for the Pilgrim to be able to experience the re-discovery of the personal voice. That's what is at the heart of choosing a writing partner and reading out loud. If one relied on a writing partner just for feedback about the words one has written then it could all be done by mail and one need never actually meet anyone else. This would be a sad loss for it is the experience of saying one's words out loud to another that is quite possibly of more value than any critical appraisal, however skilful. The Pilgrim is just finding out what it feels like to go out on her own, and this is the time when one is trying out one's voice. The development of this personal sense of who we are as writers is something that will reach a new level as we go through each new archetypal stage in turn. The Magician's calm voice will be very different from the Warrior-Lover's more confrontational insistence, for example. The chapter on working with others was placed where it needed to be so that the move from Pilgrim archetype and upwards could be facilitated, and so that the on-going use of writing partners would keep the development happening.

The plan has been entirely conscious, throughout.

When I asked you to write the 'Because' exercise it was as a way of asking you to explore your motivations, Pilgrim-like, while on a journey inwards. Coincidentally it also works well as a way of considering the outer recognitions of structure involved in finding the turning points in one's life. With luck it also led you to a declaration, of sorts, that you were doing all this writing for a reason. This is the dawning of the Warrior-Lover stage. Again, the visualization of the three gifts (or perhaps more than three) which followed the 'Because' exercise, was an invitation for you to take what you needed so that you could move forward as a Warrior-Lover. It was an exercise in which you, to some extent, could define what you needed to do and then arm yourself for the struggle ahead, just as knights of old used to choose their weapons.

The Warrior-Lover as a writer is in some ways the most challenging stage. All seems well at first, since the writer has found a task that she considers is worthy of all the effort, and sets about it with courage and determination. This is admirable. And yet the purpose of any stage is that it should be outgrown, and the way the Warrior-Lover stage unfolds is that it leads us to a form of temporary despair. This is the point where writers, if they don't know that this is only another stage, are likely to ask whether there will be any tangible pay off. Will this book get published? Will I be able to finish it? Is it worth all the effort I'm putting in? Sometimes the pressures that bring those questions to the forefront are so strong that the writer gives up. This is understandable, but, actually, it's not necessary. This is what one may call 'touching death'. The Warrior realizes that sooner or later he or she will die, and that no achievement lasts (and many aren't even recognized) so in the face of this it's very tempting to give up. This is when the Lover aspect of the archetype has to be invoked, to remind all of us in this situation that we are not doing it for the external rewards, or for the ego gratification, but for what it will do for our souls. When we see this, almost all of us agree to carry on, because it's the only game in town. In some ways one might think of it as the ultimate act of faith – the writer continues even though the illusions of fame and fortune are fading, have faded, and are no longer of any consolation. At this point we are not really in despair (which is what some people think, and thus they become depressed), but rather on the brink of real faith, where we agree to carry on with the task even if there is no obvious pay-off of a conventional sort. Finding faith in oneself like this is close to what Joseph Campbell described as finding one's 'bliss'. We do what we do because it *feels vital*, not because it can be proved to be profitable. Finding that sense of faith in oneself and what one is doing is an achievement beyond any reward. Yet so many people give up just as they are on the brink of becoming the Monarch archetype.

An artist friend of mine, who is a Monarch in many aspects of her life, gives workshops in which she describes, again and again, how budding painters come to her explaining that they gave up art in college, forty years ago, sometimes because there was no time, or because of having children, or some other very real obstacle. My friend knows what the expression is in their eyes: she describes it as the students wanting to be who she is. She can't actually turn to them and say, well, I got to be who I am by drawing every day of my life for fifty years – that would be too discouraging. But to some extent it is the continued practice and devotion, over years, even when it seemed like a useless task, which brought her to this place. Her students can get to the same place, but it may well take time. Similarly you can reach this place and, fortunately, it may not take you so long. Why? Because while the artists needed to draw every day, the Memoirist needs only to use words every day – and we all do that by talking, at the very least. Ideally the writer who takes herself seriously and who writes fairly regularly will be 'in practice' every day and so the apprenticeship will not have to be nearly so long.

If we think back for a moment, the exercise of seeing your home as a child which followed the 'Because' exercise will, with luck, allow you to develop further the split focus that permits you to recall the moment and also to see what that moment could give you in terms of adult insights. This exercise can work at many levels – and it is also an invitation to begin to see more as the Monarch archetype would see, with a more global view than the child was capable of. When this occurs it can be useful to listen to your life, again, so that the story can come through you.

This is also why I placed the exercise of the theater visualization after the discussion of the memoir's structure. The Monarch is the figure who is beginning to see the scope of the memoir, and indeed where she stands in it. This is not a task that can easily be contemplated before you've reached that point of awareness. The Monarch also has two more essential tasks – to face the Jabberwock and to access a sense of personal power in describing the event you were proud of. Asking you to choose a moment of pride and asking you to kill your own personal monster will give a sense of achievement, surely; yet I asked you for more than this. I asked you to be aware of your inner barriers to being fully yourself, and the exercises showed that you could get rid of them. Put another way, Monarchs have little trouble feeling powerful and important. As everyone is always telling them how right they are, this is not difficult for them. What they do have trouble with is knowing how their personal view of themselves may be leading them astray. That's what those two exercises were about. Unraveling this kind of inner deception brings us nearer to the Magician stage.

Clearly this careful arrangement of exercises is no guarantee that you will be able to move from level to level effortlessly, but they are opportunities to do so. One can draw the map of one's home as a child and feel bereft of comfort, perhaps, which will place you in Orphan mode if you allow it to. And you may need to remain there for a while before moving on. But if you decide to stay at Orphan level as a permanent choice then that, really, is up to you.

So what does it look and feel like to be able to contact the level of Magician? The ancient Greeks used to say that 'the muse descended' by which they meant: to those who were devoted to their creative endeavors would come, if they were loyal, a goddess who would tell them what to write and how to write it. This seems unlikely to those of us who are rational 21st century people, so I'll just give a few examples taken from a recent workshop, where writers I was working with gathered to discuss their progress. Only one person referred directly to the muse, the Greek goddess, but I think you will notice a pattern here in what they said.

"The form [of the memoir] came to me only *as* I was writing."

"Writing… caused me to recognize the form of this piece."

"What was happening with this writing was what was happening inside me. It was changing me."

"[This piece] came to me as I was driving, so I pulled over and it just came out of me."

"The poems seem to be writing themselves and I just copy them down."

"[At times like this] it's like taking dictation."

"[Writing] brought me back to my true nature, the observer."

I give you these actual unsolicited responses because I wish you, the reader, to know that whatever it is writing does, it feels for many people as if they've finally allowed a vital part of themselves, a part that perhaps they didn't know, to give itself expression. Perhaps it is just that ordinary life requires us for so many years to be someone we may not actually be, and we rediscover ourselves with joy when the chance arises. Writing, however, will get you there faster. Robertson Davies has one of his characters, who is writing his memoir, put it like this; "As we neared our sixties the cloaks we had wrapped about our essential selves were wearing thin."

Other writers in this same group recorded that the process had opened them up to an entirely different way of looking at what they were doing, in words that echo Davies':

"My buried life collided with my recent life."

"It's remarkable to me how much I don't know; scary but exciting…."

"I don't know, I can only chronicle."

I was astonished, when I heard all these comments at the conclusion of the workshop sequence, how closely they fit with what I was expecting, and hoping, that the participants might have discovered. Each comment recorded here was greeted by the other people in the group with understanding – it was not some eccentric foreign language that only a few understood. The Magic was happening for them, perhaps not all the time, but it was happening, and the necessary soul work was being done. One woman said she'd thought about giving up her job in order to write more; another revealed that she had already done so. When we're doing soul work, and know what it is, then everything else seems a little unnecessary, sometimes. Here's another comment that shows it even more clearly:

> Memoir writing really is soul work, and it does matter. Through it we find
> the peace in ourselves, we present it to others, and they find their peace. I
> realized recently that one of the most important things about memoir work
> is these opportunities to share our truth and our stories, to hold our soul
> work in the light so that others may see us and in turn see themselves. Peace
> is truly the way.   (Jean M.)

When I first read that, in an email, it took my breath away. The Magician can be many things, including a supreme craftsman, yet there is always a touch of genuine humility involved, too. It is humility that keeps us honest. It also helps to lead us to peace. Remember those words we quoted earlier of Deepak Chopra, who said: 'You can't fix the world if you can't fix yourself.' Just similarly you can't get peace in the world if you can't achieve peace in yourself first. The more peaceful you become, the more peaceful the planet can be. So please remember, the soul work you are doing is not just about you; ultimately it's about everyone.

In this chapter I've placed my cards on the table. The exercises that make up this book have not just been randomly selected. They were specifically chosen because they will, I believe, help you to move through each archetype in turn, Innocent, Orphan, Pilgrim, Warrior-Lover, Monarch, and Magician. You will experience what it is like to be in each stage and, as you do so, you will activate the energy of each archetype. You will grow not because you have been told about growth but because you have *felt it*.

Notes

1. Robertson Davies, *Fifth Business*, Penguin, 2001 (reprint), p. 228. Davies makes the point in another way, too. *Fifth Business* is volume one of *The Deptford Trilogy* (1990), each volume of which has its own 'hero'.

Chapter Sixteen

Memoir as Liberation

When I was a young lad at school in England the sort of question that tended to come up for discussion in certain classes was usually something like, 'the unexamined life is not worth living'. And the general consensus was always that life deserved to be examined because, after all, this was a school and the question seemed to demand an answer, and anyway it was much easier to find reasons to examine life than it was to find reasons not to examine it. What no one bothered to ask, though, was exactly *how* we were to make space in our busy lives to do this examining, especially as it seemed like such a good idea. We might have argued a good line in the classroom but we didn't seem to be encouraged to spend a lot of time translating that idea into actual lived existence. And so, on the whole, it remained an unfulfilled promise. One day we'd examine our lives properly, but not just now, because now we had exams to pass.

Yet almost anyone could see that the examined, thoughtful approach to life helped to create thoughtful and humane individuals who were able to access real wisdom and a compassion that was neither weak nor hopelessly idealistic. Such people clearly existed, and were admired for their qualities. Strangely enough many of these people were not where one might expect them to be. After all, if examining life was the darling activity of academic existence then why weren't our universities and colleges simply stacked full with kindly, wise teachers who put personal growth above everything else? One look at my professors at college revealed a somewhat sad bunch, some with wounded egos, striving vainly to find meaning in their personal misery. There were some good people, of course, but surprisingly few. Over the subsequent decades of my life spent in academic surroundings I can only say that the incidence of truly miserable, unreflective and self-obsessed academics seemed to increase alarmingly.

The unexamined life was just as unexamined as if the question had not been asked.

Memoir gives us, all of us, a real opportunity to examine our lives in depth, and it is not an activity that demands we have tenured professorships before we start. It might be possible to accuse memoir writers of narcissism, and surely, writing about one's life would seem to encourage unhealthy self-involvement. But that would be to miss the point. Such people are not engaging in memoir, at all, as we have defined it.

In my classes and workshops it's been brought home to me again and again that most of the memoir writers I work with are over the age of thirty, and most are women. What I'm witnessing, to a great extent, is the emergence of a whole class of people who feel that their voices were never heard, because they were too busy raising children, taking care of husbands, or parents, or trying to make ends meet because they were in the underpaid jobs that society seems routinely to offer women. Often these women had come of age during the years of the Women's Movement, only to find that now they were expected both to have successful careers and raise children, alone, and that for many of them this just couldn't be done. Something had to suffer, and often it was the opportunity to examine their lives that got left out. Simply reaching the end of each week intact was as much as many could manage, sometimes for years. And then one day, perhaps, the children left home and suddenly there was space in which to entertain such thoughts as, 'what does it all add up to?'

As these women (and some men) found their voices, and began to honor their experiences by writing about them, they broke through the silence. They saw that they were still as disregarded as they had been in the pre-Women's Movement days, to a large extent, and often considerably less well supported financially. This was true of both men and women, for men found themselves working harder for less recompense in the new age of two-working-parents-per-family. But now both groups realized they were not alone. In examining their lives and claiming back their experiences and wisdom they were doing something profoundly spiritual, and profoundly political. By political I do not mean party politics and Capitol Hill deal making. I'm referring instead to what can only be described as the most grass-roots level political discourse we can hope for – a forum where reasoning people are prepared to engage in discussions of what can only be called deep democracy, a democracy that does not seek party lines and political expediency but that focuses instead on real issues and wishes to listen to diverse viewpoints before making major decisions. When we consider, with intelligence, how we allow ourselves to be treated, and how we actually would wish to be treated, we are asking important questions that have to do with the examined life. Asking why women are not treated as equal citizens in the United States is a personal question – why do we not respect half our citizens? And it is also a larger question – why do we permit half our citizens to be treated that way? Why do we facilitate this injustice? Because we cannot pretend that we don't.

Memoir writers dare to ask these questions, and others. The woman who writes about a childhood spent in poverty and abuse is telling a personal story but she's also asking an obvious question – why do we allow children, who have no power, to be abused, exploited, terrorized, and even destroyed in this way? Why would any humane society allow that? That, surely, is a 'political' question that is also a personal question.

It just might be that memoir writing is a radical and necessary act if we are to begin to create the democratic world we deserve. As we shake off our individual shackles of hurt, despair, and trauma we can stand outside our individual experiences and ask how our world got to be this way. When enough of us ask that question, and refuse to be deflected, then we can be sure we're moving towards addressing it fully. Memoir is a first vital step.

Memoir won't save the world overnight or anything like that, but it just might, one small step at a time, move each of us who is engaged in reviewing our lives to achieve the soul work we'll have to do if we are to be thoughtful citizens. Reactive citizens we have plenty of, thank you, since reactivity is like what the doctor does with his little hammer when he tests your reflexes – you have no control over the reaction. Memoir, and the consideration of memoir, can move us to a different place in which we take account of the wider issues. That's why memoir is never a narcissistic thing to do if you are doing it fully. Self-awareness is always going to grow more compassion; self-absorption will always grow arrogance and ignorance.

Chapter Seventeen

Endings

One of the more troubling considerations for many writers is where exactly they should end a memoir. By now you should have a good sense of the phases your life has been through, so you'll have a general idea of where to end, chronologically. The problem is how do you conclude a section of your life. Should there be some sort of philosophical rounding out of the narrative, perhaps, or a few words of encouragement, of belief, or inspirational statements?

You can choose to go in that direction, and sometimes the effects can be very good, yet we should all also be wary of the desire to stretch for meanings where none might exist, or where the ultimate 'value' feels fugitive, just beyond the grasp of our ability to articulate it to ourselves. Perhaps the experiences of a life can't be reduced to a few short paragraphs. Possibly the real meaning of a lifetime hovers over the words one writes, or radiates from the mood in which one wrote them. At such times it's not the words but the atmosphere they create that matters most.

I tell my writers to worry less about the end than about the quality of what they've included. Has your memoir included moments of mystery, of beauty, and of passion? The world is, despite what some may say, a mysterious and beautiful place. Think of the magic in a baby's smile. Just a smile; so why does it lift your whole day? And think of the depths of feeling people routinely, every day, have for each other, and you'll see the true meaning of Passion, which is a profound personal attachment to someone or something, an attachment that runs in the blood and has trouble getting articulated on the lips. Mystery, Beauty, and Passion are everywhere, and quite possibly the purpose of any memoir is to move closer to these life-affirming aspects of who we are. We can always choose to move towards mystery, ugliness, and alienation, yet I'd suggest that this would hardly be a destination we'd want to spend any time dwelling in. Memoir, in the last analysis, is the record that we've been alive and are grateful to have had the experiences we've had, even the ugly ones. We learn most from the ugly ones, after all, although that learning can be hard. Why do I make this claim about memoir? Possibly because I've seen that those who have no sense of their lives as progress towards some more profound knowledge are those who do not believe in memoir, and will not ever write one. Even thinking of writing a memoir is a way of declaring that one loves this strange world we all live in – it's an act of optimism.

Where you choose to end, then, is less important than the *mood* in which you choose to close your memoir. The mood I most frequently encounter is one that is best described as gratitude. When you feel that you'll know you're close to the ending of your life story writing.

Gratitude is really a pretty good place to be. That's the nature of soul work; it brings us to a good place.

With this in mind one of the things I've noticed about endings to memoirs, essays and stories is that there are two main pitfalls to avoid. The first is the desire to end on a tidy and even a cutesy note. While this may provide an ending of sorts, sometimes hidden in this method is a desire not to be held accountable for what one has written. I worked with one woman who habitually ended her chapters with a joking aside and this raised a laugh the first few times. After that, though, the humor actually began to distance the reader from what had been described in such careful detail earlier. It is not a good idea to spend several pages describing one's hopes and dreams and then to end it with a comment that says, 'But these are just dreams and I have to wash the dishes before company comes.' It may be true, and it may be humorous, but it effectively negates all that has come before it.

The same urge sometimes appears at the end of a memoir – that desire to say that this is just something the writer has recorded for her own amusement while sitting in a rocker contemplating old age. Not only is it evasive, it's not even true. No one writes two hundred pages of memoir sitting comfortably in a rocker thinking about nothing too much more important than the scent of apples on the Fall breeze. So the ending is a time to claim your wisdom and tell the reader why it's important to know all the things she's been reading. There is, after all, a world of difference between a memoir that ends with a statement about how five beautiful grandchildren are the light of one's life, when it's compared to a statement that says those five grandchildren have been brought up to see what's right and what's not, and they'll have to use that knowledge every day of their lives....

The rule, therefore, has to be: no cutesy, no schmaltz. Use the ending to go deeper.

A second pitfall that traps many writers is the sense just as the last chapter is about to be written that there's no point in writing more, because it's all been said already. This is a strong feeling for many writers, and they may even put their memoir back on the shelf saying: well, it'll never be published anyway and I've said all I want to say, so I'll just end here. This sort of self-talk is understandable but it's not helpful.

When this occurs I urge writers to go ahead and write the last section anyway, and attempt to make connections as they do so. Reluctantly, some of them write a somewhat pedestrian ending and sit back feeling a bit deflated. The point here is that the first ending is not going to be 'the ending'. It will bring the memoir to closure so that the writer can walk away from it for a few days, mull over what it was all about, and try and get a better grip on things. This may take time. For some people it takes weeks. Then the writer can return to the script saying that there are just a few more things that need to be added....

This is the moment we've been waiting for as it is only at this time that the writer can look at the sheaf of papers and ask the difficult questions: why did I do this? Now I've done it, what might it all add up to? The aim of a good ending is not just to go through the main points again, like an undergraduate term paper, and declare 'in conclusion...' The aim of a good ending is to take the sense you have of the life you have written about and try to raise your awareness as fully as possible to understand what has gone on. One writer put it this way: "I wanted to write about my difficult childhood and my abusive parents. But what I found myself writing about was the many ways that courage can grow when it seems there is no hope, and how strength emerges from the gaps in the pavement, as fragile and as indestructible as weeds pushing towards heaven." Where you thought you were going and where you actually went may be very different, and that's worth knowing.

To some extent every finished memoir is a declaration of empowerment. It is the proof that you wrestled with the mystery of being alive and you did not give up. You didn't shrug and mutter, 'I don't know' when faced with this task, because something inside you did 'know' and wanted to make that knowing clear. In that sense the ending is the place where you can astonish your reader – and better yet, where you can astonish yourself. Like emerging on to a mountaintop after a long climb, you won't need anyone to tell you you've arrived. You'll feel different and you'll see things differently.

This is the point when you can, if you choose, acknowledge the Magician who has been inside you, inspiring you every day, and you can contact that energy fully because it's been with you all along. For the Magician archetype is the one who links earth with heaven. This is the archetypal part of yourself that takes your personal experience and connects it to important, transcendent, life-lessons that are bigger than any single person. This doesn't have to be done in any dramatic way, of course. So here's an image that may help: think of the Statue of Liberty in New York harbor. It's just a statue, its plinth planted in the soil of a new world, one of its hands raising a blazing torch. For years it sent a message to all those who were arriving on overcrowded ships, weary and apprehensive. It said, 'You are welcome here.' It's essential to remember that. It didn't say, 'You couldn't make it in your own country so now we'll let you in as a big favor to all the failures of the world.' Its message was quite other, especially to those who had experienced rejection upon rejection. The effect was to *inspire* the arriving immigrants, and that was a generous, stirring message. Dread and homesickness were transformed into something far more energetic and optimistic. That's the power of the Magician at work – the capacity to inspire – and that's the power that exists in your memoir. If you can feel that, then you can allow your life to change; and your readers will feel it, too. Your soul work will be at a new level.

And that's when your memoir will have reached closure.

Bibliography

Memoirs of Interest

Here are some memoirs that may be of interest. This list was compiled for the Blue Hills Writing Institute with the help of the participants (to whom I am most grateful), who agreed that the selection opened up possible new ideas for ways of writing. It doesn't pretend to be comprehensive or complete, just thought-provoking. Once you start reading you'll find that one book leads on to another – especially if you talk to your friends about what you've read and follow their recommendations.

Geoffrey Wolff   *The Duke of Deception: Memories of My Father*
> How does one come to terms with the memories of one's father when that person was a confidence trickster, forger, liar, and manufacturer of false memories? The companion book to this is Tobias Wolff's *This Boy's Life*. The two are brothers who barely saw each other after their parents separated when Geoffrey was in his early teens.
> Vintage, 1979, 275 pages.

J. R. Ackerley   *My Father and Myself*
> "I was born in 1896 and my parents were married in 1919." So starts the memoir of a boy's experience of his father, of his father's secrets, and of the cost of such concealments in terms of trust. Uncompromisingly honest.
> Poseidon, 1968, 219 pages.

P. D. James   *A Time to be in Earnest: A Fragment of an Autobiography*
> Based on one entire year's diary entries, 1997-98, the famous crime-writer moves between the present and the past in ways that illuminate both. Less a memoir than a way of approaching the tricky task of life assessment.
> Knopf, 2000, 229 pages.

Kurt Vonnegut, Jr.   *Slaughterhouse Five*
> "All this happened, more or less. The war parts, anyway, are pretty much true." Vonnegut's stretching of the memoir form has become famous for what it tells us about the way some fictions (and some mouthpieces of fiction) can be used.
> Dell, 1969, 215 pages.

Vladimir Nabokov   *Speak, Memory: An Autobiography Revisited*
A memoir that touches very few of the expected events and certainly not in the
expected order. In some ways it follows the movement of his mind far more than
the movement of events. Nabokov the butterfly collector, emerges. Nabokov the
author remains veiled.
1947, various editions, 310 pages.

Seigfried Sassoon   *Memoirs of a Fox-Hunting Man*
                      Memoirs of an Infantry Officer
Sassoon creates a mouthpiece, George Sherston, by whom he tells a story that is
essentially his own. We see the transformation of the fox-hunting George into
the dutiful soldier, and from there to the anti-war activist who is sent to an army
mental hospital as 'shell shocked'. Harrowing.
1930, Penguin editions are later, 350 pages and 345 pages.

Russell Baker   *Growing Up*
Fascinating, not least for the reflections Baker gives us about his first version of
the memoir, and how it took him one whole wasted draft to get to the heart of
his story – his relationship to his mother. It also deals, in the first few pages, with
the tricky and evasive nature of memory itself. Magnificent. It won a Pulitzer
and deserved it.
Penguin, 1983, 420 pages.

F. Yeats Brown   *Bengal Lancer*
A fine, atmospheric work with one of the most unforgettable openings of all
memoir: "New Year's Day, 1905. All the long way from Bareilly to Khushalgar
on the Indus (the first stage of my journey to Bannu) I was alone in my railway
carriage with two couchant lions."
First published 1930, Penguin edition 1970, 214 pages

Ester Taft Quinn   *Other Days: Memories from the Last Century*
A charming series of memories written for family and friends, centered upon
old photographs as the focus for each section. Well written, and an excellent
example of a book that can be delightful to read while conveying important
family history.
Quirk (self published), 2002, 271 pages.

David Kidd (and John Lanchester)   *Peking Story, The Last Days of Old China*
Arriving in China at age 20, in 1949, David Kidd fell in love with and married an
aristocratic Chinese woman just as Mao's Cultural Revolution gathered steam to
sweep everything away, forever. An unusual, delicate, evocation of an era moving
towards dissolution, it covers just two years that irrevocably shaped the author's life.
Reprinted 2003, New York Review Books, 208 pages

Joe Simpson   *Touching the Void: The True Story of One Man's Miraculous Survival*
Joe Simpson shattered his leg descending one of the highest peaks in the Peruvian Andes, and despite his climbing partner's help, he had to be abandoned. Alone, unable to climb, he still managed to find his way back to base-camp. It is, truly, a story of miraculous survival. It's also a great example of one defining point in a man's life.
Harper, 2004, 224 pages

Modern American Memoirs edited Annie Dillard and Cort Conley
The perfect read for memoir writers, this volume provides extracts from 35 of America's greatest memoirists, in every style, shape and size. A must-have.
Harper 1995, 450 pages

Primo Levi   *Survival in Auschwitz*
Levi's memoir of his eighteen months in Auschwitz is harrowing in every way, and yet it is less a story of horrors than an investigation into what it is that makes us human. His organizing principle is roughly chronological, but it is also, as he says, shaped by the pressure with which the events erupted into his mind after the events. Perhaps the most useful memoir one could ever read, since it is not about Levi, or his pain, so much as it is about the situation.
Widely reprinted since 1958; Touchstone Books, 1996, 200 pages

Robert Graves   *Goodbye to All That*
Graves' memoir of his growing up and service in the First World War is a classic for all time. He focuses most on his military days, showing how his whole life was a preparation for it, and how an entire nation would never be the same again.
Penguin, 1960. 350 pages.

Banjo Clarke   *Wisdom Man*
Clarke, an aboriginal growing up in the church-led settlements of Australia, relates the tale of his life to Camilla Chance. It is episodic, completely oral history based, and utterly readable. It gives us a rare glimpse into the mind and heart of the aboriginal, is never self-pitying or sentimental, and full of that rarest of all qualities, real love.
Penguin, 2002. 250 pages with many pictures.

Alberto Piranjo.   *A Cure for Serpents*
Chosen by Nobel prize-winner Nadine Gordimer as one of the must-read books for all those interested in literature, Piranjo describes his work as an Italian doctor in North Africa, working with the Bedouin until the Allied armies of World War Two came and he was interned. Piranjo is compassionate, an astute observer, and completely uninterested in self-justification.
Reprint Society, London, 1956. 264 Pages

Albert Facey   *A Fortunate Life*

Facey was approached in old age as part of an oral history survey. The resulting story proved to be a huge best-seller in Australia. Facey's life included World War One and extraordinarily hard work in the bush farms. Clear-eyed, he wastes not one word of reproach on anyone and is never sentimental. Yet the text is astonishing. Penguin, 1981, 334 pages.

Dirk Bogarde   *The Great Meadow, An Evocation*

The second in a series of memoirs written by the British actor, this book covers his childhood years during the late 1920s and 30s. Living in a remote cottage in the Sussex Downs with his younger sister, Bogarde gives a riveting glimpse of this idyllic time to be a child. Sprinkled with his sketches and with the cover illustration from a painting his father did of the cottage, it is a beautiful piece of work. Penguin, 1992, 207 pages

Roger Angell   *Let Me Finish*

Totally without rancor or sentimentality this gorgeous, elegantly written account of his early days with a remarkable father, Ernest, New Yorker editor/mother Katharine, and step-father E.B. White makes the reader agree with Roger Angell, "Yes, finish, and never stop writing." Intimate, funny, moving, fresh, a writer's memoir.
Harvest, 2007, 320 pages.

Geoffrey Wellum   *First Light*

A war memoir of a Battle of Britain pilot from 1939 to 1942. Based on notes and diaries this is a remarkable memoir that brings in the real sense of the fear and excitement experienced. He uses physical detail with scrupulous care, without overloading. For the first time in reading a memoir of this sort I felt I understood the strains of combat flying. It was a huge best seller in England, and rightly so. Penguin Books, 2002, 386 pages.

Doug Block   *51 Birch Street* (DVD)

A portrait of his parents' fifty year marriage. It explores the universal question "How much about your parents do you really want to know?" This is always an interesting question for memoir writers. The DVD is especially interesting because it includes interviews with the family members for their reactions to the whole process of sharing their story with the world, and seeing the audience's emotional reactions to the film.

Vivian Gornick   *Fierce Attachments*

Written in 1987, before the boom in memoir, and viewed as a classic of the genre, Gornick writes in a tightly controlled yet passionate way about her relationship with her mother during her childhood and well into her feminist adulthood,

manipulating time artfully in a series of punchy vignettes rather than chapters. She is a journalist and also the author of 4 other books.
Farrar Strauss Giroux, 2005, 216 pages.

Mary Lou Shields *Sea Run: Surviving My Mother's Madness*
Shields renders her life and her process through five years of psychoanalysis in language that is spare, deceptively simple, and intensely evocative. It has been used in college classrooms across the country for its clarity and insight into the workings of not only the mind, but the heart.
Seaview Books, 1981, 339 pages.

Kathryn Harrison *The Kiss*
As the NYT said, "Appalling but beautifully written . . .jumping back and forth in time yet drawing you irresistibly toward the heart of a great evil." This is the kind of book one doesn't imagine being able to read because of the subject matter; yet the writing is so searing and deft one cannot abandon the tale, or the narrator. Harrison brings so much perception and light to the darkness of incest that she gives the reader that gift only offered rarely: wisdom. She is the author of three other books as well.
Harper Perennial, 1998, 224 pages.

Dorothy Allison *Bastard Out of Carolina*
Written from a child's point of view it uses humor and telling detail to evoke the story of the girl called "Bone" and her impoverished, tumultuous life in Greenville County, South Carolina. A violent family triangle takes her to the edge within her larger, chaotic, extended family circle. The complexities of love between mother and daughter are rendered with painful freshness and truth.
Plume, 2005, 320 pages.

Ann Patchett *Truth and Beauty: a Friendship*
The author of Bel Canto writes about her lifelong friendship with Lucy Grealy, poet and author of *Autobiography of a Face*. The writing is deft. Readers come to know a great deal about Grealy, less about Patchett herself. The friendship itself, intensely loving, becomes a third character in the book. A rare and privileged glimpse into how two women's friendship can sustain and support them through change and difficulty. Patchett is the author of four novels and has received numerous writing awards.
Harper Perennial, 2005, 272 pages.

Hayward, Brooke *Haywire.*
Growing up in Hollywood, with a famous actress mother and a father who is a renowned producer, is a far cry from Father Knows Best. This was a loving family, but there were also neuroses and legacies from past marriages as well as fall-out

from the fact that life is not a script and it can't be reshot if mistakes occur. And there were mistakes. One child committed suicide at the age of 21 and her mother's life ended similarly, while a second child, a son, was institutionalized. Brooke was the strong one and has crafted a memoir of extraordinary vision which gets beyond familiarity, a tough thing to do.
Alfred A. Knopf, 1977, 325 pages.

Carrighar, Sally   *Home to the Wilderness*
This is the memoir of the renowned naturalist, Sally Carrighar, who gave us *One Day on Beetle Rock, One Day at Teton Marsh* and other studies in the field. Essentially, the author grew up motherless because her mother had been physically damaged during a difficult birth (which also partly deformed the face of the baby). The result was total rejection, a refusal by her mother to play the mother's role and jealousy if the father attempted to fulfill his parental part. But the healing power of nature was at hand and it is our good fortune that the author found it and shared it with all who read her work.
Houghton Mifflin Company, 1973, 330 pages.

Cooper, Wyatt   *Families: A Memoir and a Celebration*
"To my two families, the one that made me and the one I made" goes the dedication and it's on target. The author came from a modest Southern family and married the heiress of the Vanderbilt fortune. From that union came CNN's Anderson Cooper and his brother, Carter, dead a few years ago by his own hand before the eyes of his horrified mother, Gloria. This book is all about family dedication. Why then do such families end in tragedy no less frequently that those who are not similarly blessed? But Wyatt Cooper was long gone before the tragedy occurred and so his memoir is charming, profound, and very appealing in its recounting of two very different cultures and their union in a brief but happy marriage.
Harper & Row, 1975, 199 pages.

Willis, Jan   *Dreaming Me: An African American Woman's Spiritual Journey*
By the time Willis left her home in an Alabama mining camp for undergraduate studies at Cornell University, the harsh reality of life in the segregated South of the 1950 and 1960s had left an indelible stain on her consciousness. Confronted then with the decision to either arm herself in the struggle for human rights at home or search for the possibility of a more humane existence abroad, Willis ultimately chose peace among the burgundy and saffron robes of a Tibetan Buddhist monastery over the black berets of the Black Panther Party. What she discovered, living in a narrow temple amid sixty Tibetan monks, was the healing place she had sought but not found in her Southern Baptist town of Docena.
Riverhead Books, 2001, 321 pages.

This book is also available in paperback. The paperback title is slightly different: *Dreaming Me: From Baptist to Buddhist – One Woman's Spiritual Journey*

FINDHORN PRESS

Life changing books

For a complete catalogue,
please contact:

Findhorn Press Ltd
305a The Park, Findhorn
Forres IV36 3TE
Scotland, UK
t +44-(0)1309-690582
f +44-(0)131-777-2711
e info@findhornpress.com

or consult our catalogue online
(with secure order facility) on
www.findhornpress.com

For information on the Findhorn Foundation:
www.findhorn.org

green press
INITIATIVE

Findhorn Press is committed to preserving ancient forests and natural resources. We elected to print this title on 30% post consumer recycled paper, processed chlorine free. As a result, for this printing, we have saved:

5 Trees (40' tall and 6-8" diameter)
2,271 Gallons of Wastewater
2 Million BTU's of Total Energy
138 Pounds of Solid Waste
472 Pounds of Greenhouse Gases

Findhorn Press made this paper choice because our printer, Thomson-Shore, Inc., is a member of Green Press Initiative, a nonprofit program dedicated to supporting authors, publishers, and suppliers in their efforts to reduce their use of fiber obtained from endangered forests.

For more information, visit www.greenpressinitiative.org

Environmental impact estimates were made using the Environmental Defense Paper Calculator. For more information visit: www.papercalculator.org.